Surrounded by Love

Meva J. Scarff

authorHOUSE®

AuthorHouse™
1663 Liberty Drive
Bloomington, IN 47403
www.authorhouse.com
Phone: 1-800-839-8640

Published by AuthorHouse 05/29/2015

ISBN: 978-1-4969-5804-4 (sc)
ISBN: 978-1-4969-4201-2 (e)

Library of Congress Control Number: 2014919322

Print information available on the last page.

Any people depicted in stock imagery provided by Thinkstock are models,
and such images are being used for illustrative purposes only.
Certain stock imagery © Thinkstock.

This book is printed on acid-free paper.

Because of the dynamic nature of the Internet, any web addresses or links contained in this book may have changed
since publication and may no longer be valid. The views expressed in this work are solely those of the author and do not
necessarily reflect the views of the publisher, and the publisher hereby disclaims any responsibility for them.

CONTENTS

Tiece's Story. Early Years 5

Growing Years 7

Daddy 13

Mother 19

Great-Grandmother Johnson 25

Great-Grandmother Owens 27

Buddy Hale 31

Randy 35

Annabelle 37

Grandma Marian Johnson 39

School Days 43

My Careers 47

My Social Life 49

The Martini Years 51

My Poetry 63

My Beautiful Jim 83

The Bronco 101

Settling In 111

Thirty Years of Teaching the Three Rs 119

The Scarff Family 131

The Johnson Family 137

Six Generations of Oil and Gas 145

About the Author 151

About the Book...153

Meva Threase Johnson Scarff as a baby

Other Books by Meva Scarff

TIECE'S STORY. EARLY YEARS

Early remembrances:

Mother pulling me back through the fence between our house on the hill and Grandma's house.

Daddy carrying me on his shoulder to Grandma's house.

Daddy carrying me to get ice cream after I'd had my tonsils removed.

Mother singing.

Going to work with Daddy while he pumped his "earl" wells.

Remembrances of the "house out the road."

Playing cars with Buddy under the house and being afraid of getting "stuck" in the close space where the front room met the ground.

I was born on January 13, 1936. Mother and Daddy lived in a two-room house on my grandfather's farm. It was located on the Marshville Road in Harrison County. It had a kitchen and bedroom and a small porch. It had been built above a basement. We had an outhouse behind the house. When I was two and a half years old, I got a baby brother, Buddy Hale. He was a big baby, weighing ten pounds.

A little while after Buddy was born, Grandpa decided we had outgrown our house and traded it for a house on the other side of his. It was larger and fit us better.

Playing with Joy, my aunt, and Buddy in our "playhouse" was great fun. We had made a playhouse under the house using a crib-type projection. We put curtains on the opening to the outside, "our window." We put boxes under the inside opening to be our steps. We spent hours inside it or riding our horses (broomsticks) back and forth to it.

Our dining room had a hole in the floor that had once held a pipe. Daddy never closed it since it just went to the ground under the house. Bud and I were not lovers of beans and peas. Mother and Daddy would leave the table to go to the front porch to swing after dinner. Bud would push his peas to my plate, and I would drop our peas to the ground through that little hole. We would then go to the porch and lie through our teeth and swear we had eaten all our food. Mother told me, years later, that they knew what we were doing since she saw the results when she went down to the cellar.

Daddy had dug a large hole in the ground under the house. It was used as a cellar for our potatoes and apples. He had put board shelves in it, and I think Mother used them to store some of her canned goods. The cellar had a large board as a cover.

The back porch was a decent size, and it served as a good place to sit when the sun was hot. Mother kept her washer there. Wide steps led up to the porch, and the water pump was at the bottom. Mother hung her clothes to dry on a long clothesline in the backyard. I can remember the clothes flapping in the summer breeze. They smelled so good. The clothes froze in the winter, so they had to be brought inside to finish drying. Then Mother would sprinkle them with cool water, wrap them, and put them in a basket to wait for ironing.

Mother sang her sweet hymns on those days, and I would sit and listen and learn the words. Sometimes I sang with her, and sometimes I got the words mixed up and came up with really silly or naughty-sounding lines. She would sing, "I was seeing Nellie home, I was seeing Nellie Home. " I thought I heard, "I was born in Nellie's hole, I was born in Nellie's hole."

I sang that one time in front of Mother, and she said, "Meva Threase, what are you singing?" I sang it again, and she said, "Don't ever sing that again; it does not sound nice."

When I asked why, she said, "Just because it doesn't. So don't sing that again."

When I asked her the correct lyrics, and she told me, I laughed like crazy. I was old enough to understand the difference.

We had such good times, Mother and I. She would tell me the funny little ditties Aunt Edith (her mother's sister) would say. They were spicy, and we'd laugh and laugh. Aunt Edith was a spry old gal and could still roll down the hill when she was probably in her seventies.

GROWING YEARS

Before 1950, the house contained five rooms: a living room, two bedrooms, a dining room, and a kitchen. My brother and sister Randy and Annabelle were born in 1945 and 1946, respectively. I think the babies slept in Mother and Daddy's room at first, because I remember sleeping with Buddy when we were little. I guess Daddy decided he had to build some more rooms in 1950, because he had a new kitchen and a bath added at that time. Then Bud and Randy shared a bedroom, and Annabelle and I shared one.

We had a long front porch with a glider and chairs on it. The path from the house to the road had steps and a board walkway.

The winter Annabelle was probably four or five months old, Daddy had Palace Furniture install a new heater in the living room. That next morning Daddy got us up and out of bed really early and made us go outside. He carried the babies outside. Annabelle was limp as a rag, but was okay after a few minutes. It seemed Mother had been up with Belle during the night, or we all would have died of carbon monoxide poisoning. She was able to awaken Daddy, and together they herded us out to sweet, clean air. Palace Furniture had put the vent on backward, letting the fumes vent inside. We certainly had God watching over us that night.

There were two large maple trees in our front yard, one on either side of the steps. Each tree had at least one large branch that could hold a medium-size child, and guess who used the branches as lounges? You guessed it if you said Bud and Tiece. We spent hours in those trees looking out and dreaming of faraway things. At least that was what I did, and I suppose Buddy did the same. Those branches were an easy retreat when we were mad, sad, scheming, or just bored. I guess today's children would retreat to the TV or computer, but we had the much more exciting, I think, realm of make believe or daydreaming. I don't know when I last climbed that tree, but I think I was well into my teens.

This may be the place to explain a little of my Johnson family tree. Grandpa and Grandma were Croghan and Marion Johnson. Their four children were Glenn William (my father), Hale Everett, Marjorie Lou "Margie", and Joey Lee "Joy". Joy was only two years and two months older than I was, and although she was my aunt, our relationship really felt more like sisters. We only lived half a football field's distance from each other all those years growing up. There were other members of the Johnson family tree, but I think that is probably enough for now. I'll try to stick them in as I go along.

Joy Lee and I would sometimes go to the creek fishing with Grandma. Grandma liked to fish, I guess, as her own little getaway. It was not like it was a big river, just a small creek that was probably two feet deep at a normal time.

Anyway, Joy and I just loved to go, and when Grandma wasn't looking, we would attach crawfish to the hem of her dress. We just loved to hear her scream when they touched her legs. I suspect she knew all along what was going on and played along with us, but we thought we were being really sly. She was such a good grandparent. She let me wander in and out of her house at all hours to play with Joy, and we had such good times. We would play games like pick-up-sticks, board games, and jacks, as well as others in the backyard, such as tag and hide and seek, if we could get Buddy to join us. We played a game I think we made up. It consisted of grabbing the other person's arm and swinging her around and around and then letting go. The other person was supposed to pose as a statue. Now that I think of it, I think we called the game Statue. Anyway, the aim of the game was to make the best pose. I laugh to think how we judged our own poses as to who did the best job.

Grandpa Johnson had a cerebral hemorrhage when he was forty-nine and was disabled for the rest of his life. I think I was maybe eight or nine years old at the time. He was such a fun grandpa, and it was so sad to see him not able to respond as he had before his illness. He still would play with us, but we had to be very careful not to infringe on his rules. For instance, a slamming door would set him off in anger.

We tried to be very careful to tiptoe around for his sake. One late evening I went to their house. I was skipping around the walkway, when out of the blue someone said, "Good evening." I just about peed my pants. It was Grandpa playing one of his tricks on me. He was standing under one of the large trees in the backyard, and I just failed to see him. He got the greatest kick out of that.

The day he died, Joy and I were playing on Grandma's piano when he came into the sitting room and joined us on the piano bench. He looked at Joy and said, "You know, Joy, I think your old daddy is going to be getting well."

Bless his heart, he died that night in his sleep.

I really loved him!

Joy and I did other things that we knew were not allowed, but we were kids and we took chances. We sometimes played in the smoke house. It was in the backyard. They no longer used it for storage of meat, and it made a good place to hang around. We were in it one day when Uncle Jimmy, Grandma's brother, came to visit. As he came around the walkway to the back door, he flipped his cigarette onto the lawn. We could see him through the spaces in the logs, but he could not see us. After he went in the back door, we ran out and got the butt. It was so much fun to puff and pretend we were, oh I don't know, movie stars or some such great and grand person.

Pretence was such a creative pastime. We didn't have television or any of the sophisticated games children have nowadays. We just made our own, and sometimes they were a little hazardous.

An outside staircase took you to the basement in Grandma's house. It had a frame around it that was topped by boards about a foot wide. At the top of the frame where it met the house was a narrow board, maybe six inches wide, that went from one side of the steps to the other. Joy and I spent many hours sitting on the boards by the stairs, talking about the world, boys, boys, boys, and all other things girls would be interested in. We also did our little bit of daredevil stunts on that six-inch board that was probably ten feet off the ground. We would place our backs against the house and slip inch by inch across that board. If our mothers had seen us, they would have tanned our hides . However, our mothers were doing housewife-y things and had no idea we were taking our lives in our own hands.

Sometimes, Buddy and I would hatch up a little mischief, and when Mother found out, she would warn us that we should not do whatever it was. We would promise not to do it again. If we were caught, she would say, "The next time, you will feel the switch!" And what did we do but blunder into whatever it was again, and she would go the forsythia bush and break off one of those little thin branches. We knew how they stung, so we would start running around the house to get away from her. Our house sat on a hill, so we would really run up the hill and then down the other side, with Mother right behind us. After a while, we could see Mother getting winded, so we crouched down and accepted our lashes. They stung, but we loved Mother and didn't want her to get sick from chasing us.

Now Buddy Hale, my oldest brother, had his own brand of mischief. He and I played many times under the house. It did not have a basement but sat on the ground. It was good height at the bottom but got shorter and shorter as you edged up to the top. Bud would dig roads, and we would "drive" his little cars up and down the roads. He just loved to make up a game that would take us way up high in between the floor of the house and the ground. He knew I couldn't stand it, and he'd laugh and laugh and call me "little baby" and names like that. I would try and try but just couldn't get clear to the top where my head would be wedged between the house and ground. I was afraid the house would fall on me, and the close space smothered me. Claustrophobia, I think it's called. At that time it was just "being babyfied."

Buddy was a good brother though, and we had many fine times. We explored the hills, and a great time to be had by Bud, Joy and me was to go to the great big rocks on the farm. You could walk onto them from the pathway, and if you walked over to the end, you could look way far down, maybe as much as thirty feet.

From the bottom looking up, it was awesome. The rocks hid caves that I think foxes lived in. They had big holes that the wind may have blown out over the years. There were large oak trees standing all around the rocks. Their big branches loomed overhead as you looked up.

One time we found a large grapevine hanging down so low that we could grab hold of it. What fun it was to grab the vine, take a run, and swing way out over the rock ledge. We tried to keep this a secret from the adults, but I guess someone got curious about how often we meandered toward the rocks. Daddy told us to leave the vine alone and explained how dangerous it was to use it as we did. Now, did we listen? Do pigs fly?

One day we went up to find our beloved vine gone. We ran down home and asked Mother what had happened to it. She said she did not know, because she never went up there. We asked Daddy and he said, "You mean it's not there anymore?" He never really lied about it, he just kept taking our minds away from it. Daddies are good at things like that. At least mine was.

Years later, when I asked him what really happened to it, he told me that he and Uncle Hale had cut it down.

Daddy bought us a bike, a boy's bike. I didn't care because I just wanted to ride one, boy's or girl's. I guess they thought it would look better for a girl to ride a boy's bike than for a boy to ride a girl's. Sissy and all of that Hah! Bud was never a sissy. Grandpa knew we were a bit destructive on things, and he told someone we would have it torn up in a week. Daddy heard that and told us if we put one scratch on it, it was gone forever. Now, we were believers, and we treated it like it was gold. Bud and I kept that poor thing hot all the time. I learned to ride it while standing on the seat. I was a real daredevil.

Good thing there was so little traffic on our road, just a car or two a day for a long time. I think Bud rode that bike after he was married and hit a hole, fell off, and broke his arm.

All three of us children, Joy, Buddy and me, belonged to the 4H club and went to camp in the summer. One summer, camp was coming up in two or three days, and Joy and I went bike riding. Joy was using Margie's bike, which was a much-revered thing. No harm could come to it, or Joy's privilege would be suspended. I was using the bike Bud and I shared. Joy and I decided to see how close we could ride, and my pedal caught in her front wheel. Off the bikes we went, into the road. I imagine our hands were hurt, but the thing that really worried us was our ankles. They were cut and scraped, and we knew our camping trip was in danger. We decided if we wore our socks turned up, no one would be the wiser. I think Joy hid Margie's bike in the garage. We didn't think she would see it, since she was "too grown up" to bother with a bike anymore. I can't remember what I did with ours. Maybe I thought it wouldn't be noticed, because Bud would keep a secret. We did get away with our little accident and went to camp.

Joy and I were just little demons sometimes. We knew how frightened Marjorie was of anything that crawled. We delighted in catching a worm, spider, or anything that moved. We'd put it on a branch, and finding Marjorie, we'd sing out, "Oh, Margie, guess what we found." Then we'd lunge at her with the stick, and off she'd go, screaming and screaming. That was one of our favorite "games."

Once, Marjorie was baking a cake for my grandmother's birthday. She was busily mixing up the butter and eggs when she was called from the kitchen. Joy and I took an enormous rubber spider and attached it to the inside of the pantry doors. We knew she would have to open them for the flour she would be needing soon. What a suppressed, giggly time we had waiting. Finally, the happy time arrived. Margie opened the pantry, saw the spider, threw the mixing bowl and spoon, and screamed and cried at us, calling us every nasty name she could think of. Of course Margie's nasty words were not really bad, but we had such fun with her squeamishness.

I really loved my aunt Margie and miss her so much now that she is gone. She was always a swell sport and loved us as much as we loved her.

Joy and I, like others young girls, fell in love. Laughingly, it was with the same boy. Oh, how we longed over Danny Fox. He went to school with us (I can't remember what age he was at that time) and lived on Flinderation Road. He lived with his grandparents, and their home was about two or three miles from our homes.

Joy and I decided one afternoon to "sneak" up to see if we could get a glimpse of him. She got on Margie's bike, and I got on our big tricycle. Off we went. Joy, of course, had to lag to let me keep up. I can still remember how tired my legs got with all that pumping. Thing is, I can't remember if we ever made it clear to Danny's home. We probably got tired, or I got tired and begged Joy to go back home. I can remember going to the covered bridge, just a short way from my home, and writing our names with that of the boy we loved. Sometimes it was with the same boy. I wonder how we kept from coming to blows over that. I guess we both knew it was in vain but kept hoping.

Our school was a seventh-to twelfth-grade high school, Bristol High School. The Fahey boys went to school there too. I saw dark-haired, blue-eyed Paul Fahey and lost my little girl heart. I just mooned over him day and night for two or three years, I think. He knew I was there, but since he was about three years older, as a sophomore, how could he be interested in a paltry little seventh grader? He always remained in my mind even after he graduated. We dated a few times, but we both found others to fill in our time.

While I was mooning about, Joy was falling in love with Paul's brother, Gene. Gene was a real looker, with that same curly dark hair and brown eyes. He was such a devil. Gene went into the army, and Joy waited for him to get out and come home to her. He did that and they were married. They had a girl, Janet Lee, and a boy, Michael. They are now the grandparents of three girls and one boy.

DADDY

Glenn William Johnson was born on August 4, 1911, oldest son of Croghan and Marian Johnson. He grew up in Bristol, West Virginia, on Raccoon Run. He attended the schools in Bristol and graduated from Bristol High School in 1930. He went to Salem College for a short time.

Daddy had one brother, Hale Everett, and two sisters, Marjorie Lou and Joey Lee. He and Hale were very close. They worked together in the oil field and tried to keep the family farm going.

Uncle Hale was a real joy to me as a young child. I believe he is the person who really gave me my nickname, Tiece. He really called me Trecie, but Buddy heard it as Tiece, so it stuck. Uncle Hale died by his own hand one fall day when he was in his late-forties. His death was a real jolt to our whole family. He had problems, but we never thought it would take him into such a decline. There were so many "if onlys," but what happened happened, and nothing could erase it. Daddy had little to say but grieved very hard. His helper and lifelong buddy was gone.

Daddy would often take Bud and me to work with him. It was a really fun but tiring day. It would start with Daddy getting everything ready for his day's work: tools, lunch, water, rags for wiping dirty hands, etc. Then we'd get in the 1936 Ford car and off we'd go. Daddy would park just off the road below most of his wells and we'd walk up, up, up.

We'd get tired and Daddy would stop, turn around, view the mountains, and say something like, "Can you imagine what it took to make this old world? God sure had his work cut out for himself. Look at the mountains, how tall they are. The rocks, how big they are. Look at that valley. Did you know that it was made by that little stream you see down there running all the time for millions of years? Yes, that is what cut out the valleys."

Of course we were asking questions as fast as he could answer them, but he never got tired of answering. Then he'd start off again, and we'd follow, so excited, knowing Daddy had lots of fun waiting for us.

After Daddy got the well running, he would lift us up and let us ride up and down on the big Pitman that kept the band wheel running. He would never leave us alone for fear of our getting hurt. He would take out his pen knife and whittle us little knives out of tree limbs.

One time he took us over to the big oil tank. We climbed on top and went to the side. He told us to look over at the log that lay on the ground below. While we watched, he put the long measuring pole down in the tank and pulled it out, dripping with oil. He took it over and let it drip on the log.

He said, "Now watch what will happen." Wouldn't you know he was playing with a black snake and her babies? They all crawled out to get a little oil on their bodies. He said he did that every time he went to that well. He always told us not to kill black snakes because they were not dangerous to us and would kill the copperheads that stayed around the wells. Copperheads were poisonous and could kill you.

One time when Buddy went with Daddy, he asked if he could reach up into the big box and get the can of oil Daddy needed.

Daddy later said, "I almost said okay, but something told me not to. When I opened the box three copperheads were inside. Poor little Buddy would have been a very sick little boy. The venom might have killed him, since we were so far away from a doctor."

We would play in the woods until lunchtime and Daddy would call us to come eat. He would open a pipe that spewed oil and we washed our hands in it. Daddy said anything that came out of ground could not be dirty, so we went along with him and washed our hands in that black, greasy stuff. Then we wiped our hands on the rags he had brought and dipped into the goodies Mother had sent, usually peanut butter and jelly, or peanut butter and pickles, or peanut butter and tomatoes. Sometimes it was cheese. There would always be a good drink and some cookies or apples. When we returned home that evening, we would be really tired.

Daddy took us on so many nice little trips as we were growing up. They were not expensive, but they were full of enrichment about our state. I think we visited every state park in West Virginia. We would always take a picnic lunch and take time to walk around and hear Daddy's lesson on whatever bit of history could be gleaned from that place.

One day, when I was around nine or ten years old, Mother and I took a walk down the road to see the neighbors. As we were walking along and talking to them, I heard Mrs. Ritter tell Mother about a young girl whose father was sexually abusing her. I was stunned to think that a daddy would do such things to a daughter. Now, my father was a very loving man and took great pleasure in holding me or hugging me. After that day, I would not let him touch me in any way. I would run if I saw he was going to hug me. Mother asked me about it one time and I couldn't bring myself to explain it to her. When I turned fifteen and sixteen, and knew more about "things," I realized my loving father would never do anything bad to me. I was so sorry for pushing him away for so many years. I started going up to him and hugging him again. I think I finally told him what the trouble had been. He just loved me and took me back into his loving ways.

My father was a meticulously clean man about his body, his clothes, and his "things." When we were small and crawled around on the floor playing, sometimes a ball or toy would roll under Mother and Daddy's bed and we would go after it. Mother would always say, "Don't touch your daddy's shoes. He will be upset if you do."

One Christmas my uncle Kenny and aunt Helen came down to see us. Daddy's father had given him a beautiful pair of fur-lined suede gloves for Christmas. Uncle Kenny saw them lying on the table, picked them up, and said, "My goodness, what a beautiful pair of gloves." He slipped his hand into one and went on and on about the softness and beauty of the gloves. Daddy agreed they were nice, but he never put them on his hands again! They laid on the top of the standing coat closet as long as I can remember.

Daddy had to have shock therapy in his sixties because of depression. I went to the hospital to see him and remarked on the length of his fingernails. He always kept them trimmed and neat. I asked him if he wanted me to file them for him. He agreed that would be nice, so I went to the gift shop to see if they carried emery boards. The lady in the shop said no, they did not carry them, but she had just put a new one in her pocket that morning, and I could have it if I wished. I thanked her and took it up to Daddy's room.

I held it up and laughingly said, "See? Mission accomplished."

He looked at it and asked, "Is it clean?"

I just did the most natural thing I knew to do at that time: I lied. "Of course it's clean. Would I use a dirty anything on my sweet daddy?"

That seemed to satisfy him, and he held out his hand for the filing of his nails.

I have always believed he thought it was time to die when he retired at sixty-two.

Daddy had never had any pastimes or sidelines. He just slept, had breakfast, went to work, came home, ate dinner, read the paper, and went to bed. He was not a fixer-up man. If the screw fell out of the door, the door would sag until someone else fixed it. So he didn't even have small jobs to take up his time.

Sometime during his sixties, he began to change. He would take naps in the chair, and Mother began to notice small changes in his style. He gradually went from that meticulous man to a dirty, smelly man. He was having small strokes, and each one took a little of his personality away from him. Mother was so upset. When she would ask Daddy for his dirty clothes to wash, he refused to give them to her. He just wore the same ones day in and day out. He wouldn't bathe or get his hair cut, and he started throwing his pills away. Mother found them in the commode one day. Nothing she would try made any difference to him.

I would go down home to see them, and Daddy would talk and be somewhat the old Daddy I remembered, but he just never changed back to his old self. I went down and talked a lot to him about the years of oil and gas our family had lived in. He gave me all of the information he could remember, and it was a lot. I started a book I called Six Generations of Oil and Gas. I have most of the notes still handwritten. Someday, when I get time, I'll sort it all out and get it inbook form. Someday!

When I was in college, I had to write a theme for English. I entitled it "Profile of a Friend." It was as follows:

I have a friend whom I have known all my life. To me, he is the very essence of love and understanding. He is a fine man, and I should like to tell you about him. Physically he looks like thousands of others. He is fair of face, with light-brown hair and eyes as blue as the sky on a balmy summer day. He is a tall, slender man with a gait like that of one with no place in particular to go, and no time limit to get there. He has a calm, relaxed approach to life and is, in all things, peaceful.

My friend taught me early in life the beauties and wonders of nature. Atop a high hill we would look out over the world and be awed by the realization that it took thousands of years for nature to produce such a magnificent view. He taught me to love and respect animals and to always treat them gently.

This same friend, when I was older, would steal away with my school books to read again the world's store of knowledge. It seemed to me that his thirst for education would never be satisfied.

It has been said of my friend that "he could work at any job with any man." Knowing him as I do, I am satisfied that this saying is true. He is a mediator in all things-peaceful, gentle, and understanding.

You must realize that my friend is human and has human frailties, as we all do. He is very slow to anger, but if he has just cause, he can be forced to give way to a fiery temper. However, I have seen him really angered very few times in my life, and each time he was quick to repent and feel ashamed.

You ask who my friend is? He is the earthly instrument of my very existence, my father.

My theme ended and I got an A for the effort. I was so proud and so was Daddy. I guess he couldn't believe I was so impressed with him. I read this memoir at Daddy's funeral on January 17, 1985. I will never stop loving and missing him. I see him sometimes in the nature he loved. The trees, flowers, rocks, hills, and valleys were all Daddy's friends, and he taught me to love them. Daddy never went to church with us, and I mourned over it as a youngster growing up, but I think he was with his Master every day of his life. I know he had been baptized and grew up going to church but for some reason just never wanted to continue the practice in later life. Maybe he and God had conversations about this. I guess I'll find out someday, because I know he is in heaven waiting for me.

MOTHER

What a love she was! Frances Martha FitzRandolph was born on February 16, 1912. She was the daughter of William and Annabelle Watkins FitzRandolph. She was raised in Salem, West Virginia, and went to Salem schools. She graduated from Bristol High School in 1931. Mother had a twin brother, Franklin. She also had an older brother, John, and three sisters, Helen, Katherine, and Margaret. She and Uncle Franklin were the youngest.

My grandfather was a barber in Salem, and my grandmother was a homemaker. She developed cancer of the uterus when mother was eleven or twelve and died when mother was twelve. Grandpa eventually married a lady named Alice Brown to help take care of his large family. They were sweet people, but I never saw them very much. Travel was not so quick then as it is today. Mother's brothers and sisters meant very much to her, and I saw them as much as I could.

I used to stay weekends with Aunt Helen and Uncle Kenny Bailey. They lived in Salem. They had two girls, Emma Anne and Dorothy Helen. My cousin Dorothy was still at home then, and I had fun being around her. I spent some time with Uncle Franklin and Aunt Mabel at their home in Grafton. My cousin Betty was at home then, and we also had good times together. Aunt Katie and Uncle Leon Canfield had two children, Mary Jane (Janie) and Leon Jr. (Sonny). They were both nearer my age, and we had great times when they visited us. They lived in Rochester, New York, and would visit every summer. Aunt Margie and Uncle Frank Smith lived in Marysville, Ohio, and we would visit them occasionally. They had one son, David. He and I were really close and had good times when we could.

Randolph Family in 1952

First Row John and Franklin Randolph
Second Row Helen Bailey, Margaret Smith, Katherine Canfield and Frances Johnson

I really had a good extended family, and we loved each other very much. There was never any bickering that I knew of. It just all seemed to be one great life. Uncle Franklin drank when I was little, and Mother banned him from her home. When I was about ten, he reappeared and was part of our family again. I guess he had changed his ways and asked Mother's pardon, and loving him as she did, she said yes.

As I have said in many ways, love was a big part of my life. I experienced it from all directions. I guess that may be why I am such a loving person. Love groomed me from childhood. I wish every person could have the lovely growing up years that I had. I thank God every day for those people.

Over the years, several family members on Mother's side died from different forms of cancer. Her older brother, John, of bone cancer. Franklin of colon cancer. Margaret from lung cancer. My cousin Emma Ann of breast cancer. My cousin Leon Jr. of melanoma, which metastasized into brain cancer. My cousin Betty of cancer of the rectum, which metastasized into brain cancer. My aunt Mabel, Franklin's wife and Betty's mother, of breast cancer.

This span of serious diseases took a toll on Mother. I think she was always waiting for the sky to fall on her. She had a bad time with her stomach when she was in her late fifties, and her doctor told her he thought it was cancer. She took the news as well as she could and went to the hospital for the needed surgery. It turned out to be diverticulosis, and he removed a length of her colon. How happy we all were that she was well!

My mother was such a good woman. She did everything to the words or hum of a hymn. She worked hard to keep us clean, fed, and happy. She and Daddy did not have very much in the way of wealth, but they saw to it that we had everything we needed. She was a stay-at-home mom, as most mothers of that day were. She worked from morning to night and sang her way through every chore. She cleaned, cooked, canned, and sewed clothes for me, and it seemed just so easy to me, looking on. I know now as an adult that she must have been exhausted, but she never complained.

We did not have running water until 1950, so her work was doubly hard, what with carrying water up and down to the kitchen. On weekends, the washtub was brought up to the kitchen and filled with warm water, and we got our weekly bath. Other days we had a sponge bath at the kitchen sink. In 1950, Daddy had a new kitchen and bath build onto the house. An electric pump was installed where we had the hand pump, so we were living in high heaven. Even the old outhouse was no longer needed. I am sure Mother's work became easier then.

Mother always got us up and ready for church on Sunday. We attended the Bristol United Methodist Church in Bristol, West Virginia. My grandfathers Holden and Johnson had given a large chunk of money for the building of the church. Mother sang in the choir and had a beautiful alto voice. She could harmonize with anything you sang. I think I inherited my singing voice from her. She loved the church and all the things it represented. She was faithful to her God and loved him with all her heart. She treated all people, especially her family, as if they were angels.

At times she was not treated that way. She wanted to be part of groups but for some reason was slightly shut out. It was as if they felt she was not socially as good as they were. If they had only known what they were doing to her. But she bore it because she loved so much. She had no selfishness in her heart. I know it sounds weird, but at times I think I see a shadow, and when I turn and nothing's there, I really think it's my mother looking over me.

Mother had dementia in her later years, and we had to put her in a personal care home. Bud and Randy were trying to care for her, Bud in the morning and Randy at night, but it got so we were afraid to leave her for a moment. I was several miles away and could not be there very much. My sister Annabelle and her husband, Chet, would often come in from Aberdeen, Maryland, and did so many things that made her life better or more cozy.

She loved to walk the road in front of her house. She once got caught in the barbed-wire fence when she stepped over for a flower. A neighbor passing by saw her predicament and helped her back across the fence. Another time she walked to the covered bridge and fell into the big stones in front of the bridge. She got up and returned home. I guess she must have looked in the mirror and seen her poor bruised, bleeding face. She put Band-Aids all over it. Randy saw her in a window and found out what had happened. She wasn't really sure what had happened, but he pieced her thoughts together and figured it out.

Bless her, she loved people, any people. One day while she was walking, a new neighbor stopped to say hello. They had seen her walking every day and thought they would introduce themselves. They talked, and she noticed they were dressed to go somewhere and mentioned it to them. They said, yes, they were going to Salem to some event. I don't remember what it was.

Well, Mother being Mother said, "I'd sure like to go there."

So, being a kindly couple, they said, "We'll be happy to take you with us."

So Mother just climbed into their car and took off with them.

When Randy came in from work and made his daily check, he couldn't find her. At first he wasn't too upset because she would wander around all the time, but the longer he looked, the more upset he got. Her purse was in the house, as was her coat. He called everyone he could think of, even me ten miles away, and could find no one who had seen her. I got in my car and drove down to Marshville to see if I could help find her.

All kinds of horrible thoughts were in our minds. Police and emergency cars were called, and the road was swollen with people trying to help or just looking. My nephew Tony and I had driven my car up the road to try to see her. As we were standing along the road, a car passed us, and I saw Mother inside. I called to Tony, and we got back in our car and followed them back to the house.

I went over to the car Mother was in. Being so upset, I really reacted badly. I bawled those people out for taking my mother with them. I dragged her up the road and into the house and tried to explain why we were so upset. She didn't understand why we were carrying on. They were just nice people who took her to Salem. I later called them to apologize. They were so sorry.

After that, we decided we had better get her some help. Not finding anyone to come into the house to care for her, we decided on a personal-care facility. My heart just bled each time I visited her. She wanted to go home, and I knew she couldn't.

She would ask me, "Which way is home from here?"

I'd tell her and then find out she had really tried to get off the porch to go home. She became ill in January, went to the hospital, and died there on January 14, 1997. My blessed mother is also waiting in heaven to see me some day.

GREAT-GRANDMOTHER JOHNSON

Hattie Lee Holden Johnson was my great-grandmother on my daddy's side. Great Grandpa Johnson had died in 1931 before I was born. Grandma lived in a big house in Bristol. Her house had many rooms, ten I think. There were two stairways, one in the rear and one in the front of the house. It was so much fun to run up and down those stairs. She had a pantry, where she made her famous sugar cookies. Boy, what a treat to go with Daddy to work and stop in to see Gramma Brissle (as we called her). We called her that name to keep her separated from Grandma Johnson (Daddy's mother). I think the Brissle came from not knowing exactly how to say Bristol. She would always have cookies and milk for us. Daddy always talked about those cookies, how they were just heavenly.

Sometimes I would go to her house and stay the night. It was such fun. She and I would do things together, and she would show me how to do things I did not know how to do.

One day she said, "Meva, we need to take care of the new kittens that are up under the wash house."

I was so excited! What were we going to do? She being the practical woman she was put them in a bag with a big rock. As we were walking out the path to the creek, I asked her what she was going to do. She said she was going to put the bag in the water.

I said in a big voice, "Gramma, they'll die."

She said yes they would, but that was what you had to do or you would have hundreds of cats hanging around.

I was appalled, but I figured she knew what she was doing. That was something I never forgot.

Joy and I would sometimes go to her house together. She had an outside washhouse. It was equipped with old but still useable appliances, a stove, a refrigerator, counters, dishware, and flatware. Joy and I just loved to play house in it. We would pick greens and cook them. I don't know if Gramma ever knew what we were doing, because we did try to keep it a secret from her. She probably would have grounded us from the washhouse.

She taught me how to play dominos. Double dominos! She had a little hand, but she would get all those pieces lined up on her palm and off we would go. I figure she probably won most of our games, but I didn't care, it was just the fun of being with her that was the joy.

Nighttime was such a thrill for me. I would get my bath, get in my pj's, and then get in Grandma's bed. She would take her long hair out of the knot that she wore by day. She would let me brush it and play with it. When we got sleepy, we turned out the lights and snuggled in.

My first night I wouldn't get much sleep, because she had clocks all over the house that pealed or rang or bonged, one somewhere on the quarter hour; one somewhere on the half-hour, and then one in her bedroom that bong-bonged loudly on the hour. What with those clocks and the trains whistling on the crossing not far from her house, I arose a wide-eyed zombie.

She would smile and say, "You get used to it eventually."

When our family visited Grandma, we would sometimes sit in one of the swings on her front porch. Her porch ran around two sides of the house. Daddy would sit on one side, me in the middle, and Grandma on the other side. They would talk and talk. I would try to say something but could never get into their conversation. I learned to wait until they had to take a breath, and then I would jump in. They would laugh and never told me I was being rude. I guess they realized I just needed to vent my spleen.

My grandpa Johnson died in November 1949, and Grandma Brissle, his mother, died three months later. I was a sophomore in high school. I always thought she just grieved herself to death.

GREAT-GRANDMOTHER OWENS

My grandmother Johnson's mother lived above the railroad tracks in Bristol. She was Amanda Lee Owens, and we called her Nan. She was a sweet, roly-poly lady who laughed all the time. Joy and I spent some time there with her and had good times. We would go out to the deep well and pull up a bucket of water by a rope. We walked up the railroad tracks to Bristol and go to the store for her. She told us many stories, and we laughed and laughed.

My aunt Maggie Nicholas stayed with her. She was a real hoot. We really liked her.

Grandma Owens lived until I was twenty-one. She died in December 1958. A sad time.

Great-grandmother Amanda Elizabeth (Lee) Owens

Amanda "Nan" (Lee) Owens

Margaret "Maggie" Owens

Margaret "Maggie" Owens and Irene Owens

BUDDY HALE

My brother Bud was my sidekick. I played with him, fought with him, grew up with him. We enjoyed each other and battled the world together sometimes. We helped Daddy in the garden at times but hated it. It took so long and was tiring. We would hang around in the big barn when Daddy milked the cows. We hung around the neighbors when they came in the summer to put up our hay into big stacks. We would go on the hill to see what was new there. We climbed the oil derricks-me only a little way, though. We went fishing in that little creek behind the house.

I remember when Buddy was about six or seven years old, he had a hard night's sleep because of a bad stomachache. I went to school the next morning, but Buddy was kept at home. I thought about him all day and worried what could be wrong.

That afternoon, on the bus, as we were returning home, someone asked me where Buddy was and I blurted out, "He might be in the hospital, "'cause he was really sick last night."

Now, I think I was just trying to be "big" with my horrible idea. Horror of horrors, when I got home I found out that my Buddy really was in the hospital. He had needed to have his appendix removed, because it was near bursting. Mother and Daddy had called Dr. Edison Ritter, our family physician. He'd driven to our house, examined Buddy, and established the need for surgery. He took Buddy to the hospital in his car, stopping on the way to pick up his father-in-law, Dr. Hudkins, who lived in Wolf Summit. They proceeded to Clarksburg and did the needed surgery.

When I went to see Buddy that evening, I was so happy to see him sitting up and smiling at everyone. I told myself he might have died because of my silly story.

Bud was three years behind me in school. We looked out for each other if the occasion arose. One day I was in the library when we all heard sounds of fighting. We all went to the windows and looked to the front of the building. Down there was my brother and Bob Furner, a little shrimp of a guy compared to Bud, trading punches.

I threw up that window and yelled, "Bobby Furner, you'd better not hurt my brother."

The skirmish ended pretty quickly. I can imagine Bud's ego was raw. I don't know if it was just not too important, or if they thought the principal might find out. Looking back, it was really funny, but I loved Buddy and didn't want anything to happen to him.

One time we went to the "Tip-Top" in Salem, West Virginia. It was a place where all the kids from Salem and Bristol would hang out on Saturday nights. We danced and had a good time. One night, a man-he was a friend but for the life of me I can't remember his name-danced with me. The dance was one in which you went "'round and "'round. I got so sick that Buddy had to pick me up and carry me to the car. Motion sickness, I guess. But my Buddy didn't let me down in time of need. He has always been there for me even after I was married and having problems. He is one of the great loves of my life.

When Buddy was sixteen or seventeen, he joined the National Guard. He had to go to camp in the summer. While he was away, I asked if I could use his 30 Ford Coupe until he came home. Now Buddy really liked that car, and he thought long and hard about my using it. I promised I would treat it as if it were my own. He finally said yes, and I was in heaven. All I had to drive before that was Daddy's 36 Ford, and that wasn't very often.

Bud went off to camp, and I carefully drove his car. One evening, before Bud was to come home, I had been to Salem. As I was attempting to turn down Marshville Road, I put my arm out to signal for a left-hand turn. There were several vehicles coming toward me on a two-lane bridge. Behind me was a cute pink Mercury convertible with two girls in it. As I watched for a chance to turn left, I saw, in the rear-view mirror, the girl in the car behind me starting to pass.

I thought, What is she doing? Can't she see the line of cars coming toward us?

Boom! We were struck from behind by a tractor trailer. I ended up across the left lane and two lanes of the small country road, heading into the embankment of the railroad. I was senseless for a couple of minutes. I really don't remember who took me out of the car. All I can remember is looking at that poor left rear fender and thinking, Bud is going to kill me.

The girls in the Mercury weren't hurt except for one cut finger. It seems the man driving the Fall City Beer tractor trailer, loaded with thirty-six thousand pounds of Fall City beer had seen a buddy of his in the log cabin lot and looked away to blow the horn and wave. When he turned back to the road, there was that pink car turning into the middle of the road. He hit her car on her left rear fender, and she hit my car with her front right fender. Bud's car had a flattened left fender.

I was so sore that I had to roll out of bed for days. I guess that was my first whiplash, of which I have had several. Bud, bless his heart, took the news with real "stuff." He was just so happy to see me whole. He got his fender fixed up, and that was that. I never drove his car again.

In 1956, Bud started dating Patty McIntire, fell in love, and in April 1957 got married. They had two children, Jimmy and Judy. Both are such sweet and caring people.

RANDY

Randy came around when I was about nine years old. Oh, that little redheaded doll. That is just what he was when he was little. Joy and I played with him as if he was our little doll baby. We would dress him up and take him on rides in his baby carria. We once pushed him down the road and left him sitting in the middle of the road. And just for fun, we walked away and sang out, "Bye-bye, Randy!" He cried so hard his little face was beet red under that little white cap he was wearing. We quickly ran back, hugged and kissed him, and quieted him. That was all good then, but he paid us back later, as he grew up, with his mischief.

Mischief-maker should have been his name. He tried everything he could to play tricks on you. He scared Margie one night as she got out of her car in the garage. He would jump out and yell or something like that. Once, Mother sent me to Grandma's for some eggs. Grandma put them in a bag and I went skipping out the road on my way home. Out of the weeds came Randy with a roar, and the bag of eggs were ready for an omelet.

Ornery as he'd been, I love my Randy. He is another one of my protectors. He would do anything in his power that I asked him to do. He loves me too, and we can be at ease together. Randy and I both resemble Daddy. Both of us are somewhat like him too. Randy stands, walks, and moves like Daddy did. We both are persnickety about our possessions. I guess it's a good thing we had a loving father.

In 1973 he started dating Pamela Barrett and found out he couldn't live without her. So in 1974, they were married. They had a son, Chad, the year Jim and I were married, 1975. Tina followed in a couple of years and Tony in a couple after that. Nice family!

ANNABELLE

Mother and Daddy hadn't really expected Randy, so when he was around two years old, they decided to have a playmate for him. His playmate turned out to be a sweet little girl. We called her Belle. She had Mother's brown eyes and patient personality. Joy and I played with her too. I guess we were the babysitters but never thought of it that way. They were just toys to us. We would dress her and cuddle her.

When Belle got out of her baby bed, she started sleeping with me. I just loved having her there. Sometimes though, I would put her in agony by pushing her with my foot toward the wall. When she could go no further, I would call out, "Mother, tell Belle to get off my side of the bed."

Of course Mother would come in, and by that time I would be all cozy on my side of the bed. Mother caught on to that game quickly and would tell me to leave my little sister alone.

Belle and I have been great friends through the years. My sister is a beautiful, doe-eyed enchantress type. She has light-brown hair and dark-brown eyes. She is six feet tall and very graceful. She has a delicate touch in all things. She chose art as her expression, and I can't think of anything that could have been more "her." I have always confided in her and she in me. She is such a settled person, while I am kind of a fly-by-the-seat-of-the-pants.

Annabelle attended Salem College and applied for a job in Maryland. Ha! To our surprise, our little girl was hired in Aberdeen, Maryland, to teach art. We all knew how quiet and shy she was and thought she would never be able to stay up there, so many miles from home and all of her family. She has told me there were times when she wished she were home, but she persevered and made herself some lifelong friends.

I think she'd been teaching at Aberdeen High School for a year or two when she met this handsome history teacher, Chester Thurlow. He really was a hunk-tall, well built, dark hair and eyes, and a handlebar mustache. You could tell he knew his way around the park. They fell in love and after some time got married. They are like two peas in a pod. They share so many characteristics. It is cute to watch them. What she starts, he finishes, and vice versa. They're both so calm in their movements and actions. "Slow and steady gets "'er done," as the expression goes.

I wish we could live closer so we could do things together, but that's not to be.

GRANDMA MARIAN JOHNSON

Grandma was a special kind of lady. She was soft but could be tough. She was nervous about so many things but could go on if needed. When I was small, I loved to be around her. She amazed me with the things she did. She'd tie a chicken to the clothesline and twist its neck off. Ugh! What a masculine thing to do, right? But you should have seen her when she was off to town for the day. All sweet smelling, wearing her diamonds and furs. She was very sophisticated.

When I was around eighteen, Margie and Grandma decided to go on vacation. They had decided Ocean City, New Jersey, would be a good place. They asked me if I wanted to accompany them, and not being a fool, I said, "Yes, yes!"

Uncle Hale had explained to Margie how to get through Baltimore (straight through, no turning off anywhere.) Well, Margie got her hammer and put it under the seat (for protection). Grandma and I got in the 41 Ford Convertible, and we were off. We stayed in Frederick, Maryland, the first night, and then proceeded into Baltimore the next day. Following Hale's instructions, we went straight through the city-and right into the animal auctions. There were so many black people, and Margie and Grandma just knew we were going to die right there. I can still see Margie rolling her window down an inch, picking up her hammer, and calling out, "Can you please help us?" Someone came over and laughingly told her how to get out of that mix-up.

We went on to Ocean City and had a really good time. When we went to the beach, Grandma would put her chair right at the edge of the surf so she would get wet a little at a time. She warned me to not go off anyplace, for she would never be able to talk to Daddy again if I got lost. I promised not to do anything so stupid.

One afternoon, I took my blanket back a little ways, spread it out, and lay down to "suntan." I never thought to tell Margie and Grandma I was moving a little for more space.

I fell asleep and was awakened by someone crying, "Please help us! She's gone. I just know she's in the ocean!"

I sat up to see what was happening, and guess what? My aunt Margie was directing the lifeguards to get out their boat and put it in the water.

I got up and went down to Grandma, leaned over, and said, "What's going on?"

She looked up at me and said, "Oh, thank God, you're alive." She yelled, "Margie, Margie, here she is!"

Margie ran over and yelled, "What have you been doing? Don't you know we thought you had drowned?" Then she hugged and hugged me and cried. I felt so bad!

Later, as we talked about it, we laughed and laughed, but it could have been tragic for many reasons. Grandma could have had a heart attack. She already was a nervous person and could have had a nervous breakdown. Who knows?

I met some really cute bellboys and even had a date with one of them. He was really nice. I've forgotten his name, but the memory is still with me.

When I was younger, Grandma would take me to town with her and Joy. We always went to Wells-Haymaker. It was a drug store, but they had a small concession stand where they made the best chocolate milkshakes ever. Grandma would always get each one of us a big milkshake. Boy, the memory of those shakes still makes me hungry!

Grandma would sometimes go visit her neighbors. Joy and I begged to go with her, and she almost always allowed it. One of her neighbors was Mrs. Murphy, who lived on Flinderation Road, just half a mile from our homes. To get to her house though, you had to walk across a swinging bridge. Grandma was terrified of that bridge. It might fall, or it might get to swinging too hard. Joy and I, as I have said before, were little demons, and we'd wait until she got to the middle of the bridge and we'd start it swinging from side to side.

Grandma would squeal her little "ooh, ooh," and we'd just giggle and giggle. She'd say, "Girls, you're going to make me faint. Please stop." So we'd stop and apologize and we would be loved again, until next time.

Grandma did what was needed to be done, always. When my grandfather started having "spells," she hung right in there, always taking care of him first . His "spells" were bad and left him almost comatose. He was having cerebral problems, but I don't think it was looked at as that in the beginning. When he was taken to Duke University, they found some things that pointed to really bad health.

When he was forty-nine, he had a cerebral hemorrhage. He lived, but he was very handicapped mentally. He had lost his ability to read, and that plagued him. He was a proud man, and to have lost that ability was devastating. I remember we would take a newspaper up to him and show him the large headlines. He tried to read those and sometimes was able to, or a least he could get a word or two. I'm not sure if it was sight loss or the brain not being able to sort things out any longer. He kept trying though, and we loved him more and more because of that.

SCHOOL DAYS

I started school when I was five. The cutoff date in 1941 was February 1. Joy was in school, and I was happy and excited about going, but when I got there, I was not so sure. Bristol Elementary School sat up on a long set of step, high on the hill. It was large and all so different. I remember, sometime during the first day, I got up, went outside, and sat down on the wide top step leading to the highway.

After a while I heard a deep but soft voice say, "Hey, little girl down there. Where are you going?"

I looked up and saw a big man with dark hair and a big smile. I said, "I'm ready to go home."

He laughed and said, "Well, you can do that later, but you haven't even eaten your lunch yet."

I reluctantly got up and trudged back into the school, his hand on my back. He told the teacher he had found a little lost sheep outside and everyone laughed. That made it better, and so my awakening to real life had begun.

I had several friends in first grade who went along with me all through school. Shirley Hickman lived on Cherry Camp Road. She wore a big box on her chest, and I learned she was deaf and needed it to hear. Over the years, that box changed many times, always getting smaller and easier for her to wear and be comfortable with. She always had trouble talking so as to be understood. When she was an adult, she got married, went away, and somewhere along the line, she got up-to-date help and speech therapy. She now speaks almost perfectly, and those days of fumbling with her speech are over.

Hugh Siders lived in Bristol. He was always fun to play games with. Just a boy. One of many of those who pestered me to death. He taunted me clear through school. I think he always wanted to be closer to me, but I always pushed him away. He was likeable though, and we got through school as good friends.

Richard Fox was in my first-grade class. He was always bringing things to school to show off.

One morning he brought a bag of beans. He showed them to me, and I yelled out, "There is a brown bean in there!"

The teacher called me to the front of the room and said, "Meva, you need to learn not to speak out all the time. Maybe this lesson will help."

She had me to go to the board, and after she had drawn a large circle on it, had me to stand with my nose pressed over it. She deliberately put it higher than my nose would fit, so I'd need to stand on my tiptoes.

After a while my little calves gave out, and I cried, "This is too hard to do."

She told me I could go to my desk but to remember that lesson. And I did! That doesn't mean I quit talking. I just watched my timing better.

Juanita Kerns lived on Cherry Camp and became a good friend. Johnny Carter lived on Raccoon Run and was another one of those pesky boys. Edward Ashcraft , Richard Samples, Donna Golden, Dorothy Bumgardner, and Eva McGary are some of the kids I remember. They all played their own roles in my elementary school years.

I had some good teachers in grade school, but I was terrified of Mrs. Nicholson. She was very thin and had wiry black hair and an index finger that seemed to go into your chest when she pointed at you. She sent me to my only spanking in school. We were having art class and weren't to be talking to each other. Flemie Whystell asked Juanita Kerns for a certain color crayon. She didn't have one but whispered to me and asked if I had one. I nodded yes, and she told Flemie I had one.

Mrs. Nicholson heard her and thought it was me. Mrs. Nicholson had a way of remembering how much we talked in class. She put our names on the board for the first offence, and a checkmark for all others. Six marks and you went to the office where Mr. Lanham, the principal, would administer the paddle.

I had four marks, and Mrs. Nicholson put another one by my name, making five marks.

I said, "Mrs. Nicholson, I didn't say anything. That was Juanita."

She replied, "Oh, so you want another mark?" and she put up my sixth mark. She said, "I guess you know what that means, don't you, Meva?"

I said, "Yes, ma'am!"

She said, "You can go now for your punishment."

So I went to the office, where Mr. Lanham spanked me two or three times. I never had another spanking, but I'll always remember that one. Oh well. I probably deserved many over the years, because I had a mouth that never slowed down, but fortunately most teachers just let it go.

I took dance and clarinet in grade school. I loved both of them but never pursued dance. I did take clarinet until eighth grade, I think.

When I entered seventh grade, I was in love: with the school, with the people, with the feeling of being big, with my classes and the different teachers. Oh so in love. I continued to love school, to the very end, even as a college student. I think I must have inherited much from Daddy-not only my build, posture, face, and hands but my love of knowledge. He and I both wanted to swallow up everything in books. I was a good student and tried very hard to always do the correct things. I made good grades in all of my schooling. Education just seemed to come easily to me. That love paid off.

Now, in high school (grades seven through twelve), I learned to know everyone, and they came to know me too. I learned after I was out of school that my home economics teacher, Edith Tucker, was really a distant cousin. I don't know why someone didn't make me cognizant of that; maybe they thought I might take advantage of the relationship. I just don't know. Anyway, I really liked Mrs. Tucker. She was so prim and proper, never a hair out of place. She taught me to sew and cook, and it really came into good use as I grew older. I sewed a lot of my clothes and had things I otherwise couldn't have afforded.

I had a lot of friends, and as the years passed, we did some silly things. When we reached driving age or just about, we would skip school and drive around the county. No place far or big, but just around. We'd laugh and do silly things, like trading places with the driver while the car was in motion.

One time Hugh was driving, and he asked me if I wanted to drive. I said sure, and as I scooted over, he slid under me in the other direction. The car continued to move, and I drove for a while. It was just a prank, but I realize now how dangerous it could have been. I think we were probably on a country road without much traffic, but still, we shouldn't have done that. All the kids in the car thought it was really something, but no one else wanted to try it.

I took part in almost every extracurricular thing that was offered. I sang in the mixed chorus, I was a cheerleader, I played girls basketball, I was a member of the Salem-Bristol Band, and I was a member of the Thespians. I was on the yearbook staff, a member of the Commercial Club, Y-Teens, class treasurer, Library Club, and the Sub-Deb Club. In a manner of speaking, I was very busy!

I prepared myself for working by taking shorthand, typing, bookkeeping, and filing. I especially liked bookkeeping.

I earned the nickname "Legs" one day when I cleared the stack of five steps to the upstairs closet. There were several people sitting on the steps, and I just jumped over them. Oh, to be young again!

One of my special friends was Johnnie Dennison. He lived at Marshville. Johnnie was a really cute boy, and I flirted with him all the time. He would tease me, but since he was a little older, he never really got serious with me. After high school, Johnnie joined the navy and was gone much of the time. When he came home on leave, he would occasionally stop at the house to say hi. Sometimes we would go out to a movie or just drive around and talk. I wrote to him all of the time he was in the service, and he would reply and sometimes send me little things from afar. After he spent twenty years in the navy, he came home. By that time I was married, so our relationship became just friends. He took a job with the US Postal Service and spent twenty years there. He got married in the 1970s, and he and his wife had a late in life child. She was born in 1978. I see Johnnie from time to time at gatherings. We are still good friends and share stories.

MY CAREERS

After I graduated from high school in 1953, I thought about going to college, but I didn't think Daddy would have the money for it, so I just went to work. I started working for Harrison County Court Judge Robert Ziegler that fall. I was his receptionist/stenographer. I enjoyed being the receptionist, but my shorthand skills were not the best, and after three months, I asked Mr. Zeigler to let me resign. He laughingly said, "I think you've made a good decision. I've enjoyed having you in my office, but I think you really might be happier somewhere else."

So I left my legal "career" and applied to the Christ Episcopal Church as secretary. I really enjoyed working for Mr. Bowie, the pastor. He was a real case. He had been editor of the St. Alban's newspaper before going into the ministry. He was a good man and a good pastor, but he had that streak of the devil in him. He was married to Anita Bowie and had three incorrigible boys, Chip, Bill, and Pete. Pete at that time was about five years old, and I held him on my lap and read to him or sang to him.

One day Mr. Bowie sent me to the parsonage for something. When I walked into their sitting room, I was shocked to see holes the size of nickels in the wooden arms of the couch. When I asked him what caused that, he said the boys took his drill and drilled holes into the arms. He just laughed as if that was everyday. And I expect it was.

Mr. Bowie had a large desk and mine was smaller. The parishioners bought him a new leather chair, and it was too short for his desk. He asked me if I minded making a switch. I said I would do whatever he wanted. He and the custodian moved his desk into my office and started to lift up my desk. Now, mine was a secretary's desk with a shelf that pulled out and up to hold my typewriter. I never thought to remind him of that shelf.

They decided to lift the desk and turn it to its side to get it through the door. Mr. Bowie was on the end with the sliding drawer. When they turned the desk to its side, the shelf came bounding out and up and caught his middle finger in the drawer. The desk was dropped, and Mr. Bowie swung himself "'round and 'round, shouting damn, damn, damn! blood flying everywhere!

I know my mouth dropped open, for a preacher just didn't use that kind of language. Of course I forgot about all of his years on the paper, which must have given him a good dose of all kinds of language. Poor soul! He was in a great deal of pain and ran immediately across the street to Dr. Evans's office. He got his finger fixed and came back to the parish house in a dour mood. He looked at me and said, "I'm sorry for the language, but at times I just have to vent."

He would write his sermon and ask me to proofread it sometimes. He had a real way of writing about the gospel. He was sincere and loved the Lord. He just had to get devilish sometimes, and he usually took it out on me. I loved him like a dad. I stayed with him until I was married in 1957, and then I resigned my job.

MY SOCIAL LIFE

I really didn't have much of a life-that is, a social life! Oh, I dated some. I had some friends from around home who I went to school with. The summer of my graduation from high school, I was offered a small job helping Executive President Bond transcribe his life with Salem College. I walked one mile to Route 50 each morning and was picked up by four guys going to summer college. They were nice young men, Pete Perri, Sam Devono, Louie Rochiesan, and Al Castellano. They would bring me to that same spot, and I would walk home in the afternoon. I have remained friends with them all of my life. Sam and Louie became teachers.

Pete was dating Janice Coffman. Her brother, Lyle Coffman, played football at Salem College, as did Pete. Lyle and I kind of had eyes for each other and would drive out for a milkshake or movie now and then. Sue Edgell's father ran the movie theater in Salem, and at times, Sue ran the ticket booth. I guess she met Lyle there, and they had a date one night. That really made me crazy; she had no business bothering my Lyle. Hah, what did I have to say? I was pushing in on his relationship with Janet Pigot.

I really liked Lyle, but his attention was mostly on Janet. Through Lyle, I met Louie Underwood. Since Lyle wasn't that interested in me, I started dating Louie. Louie was a nice guy and had a very nice family. I was at their house a lot. His mother and dad really liked me, and his sisters, Rosalee and Annalee, were fun to be with. They both dated the boys they would eventually marry.

Louie asked me to marry him at Christmas in 1955 by giving me a large, emerald-cut diamond ring. It was beautiful. I said yes and we continued to date and think about marriage.

At this time, I was working at the Episcopal Church. At lunchtime, I usually went to the Central Restaurant. It was located on Pike Street, across from the post office. My friends Barbara and Beverly Linsbeck and Nina Pasternak would meet me there for an hour of eating, laughing, and discussing what we would do that night. Jack Merandi ran the restaurant and knew all of his customers personally. He told me one day that if I didn't have that diamond on my finger, he had a great guy who was interested in meeting me. I laughed and said I guessed it was just too bad.

Louie and I dated, but I was beginning to feel that he just was not the type of man I really wanted. He was a stay-at-home type, no energy, not a lot of interest in things I was interested in, and I finally told him I was sorry but I just couldn't see myself married to him. He was upset but took back the diamond ring.

One day in the fall, I was at Central again for lunch, and Jack noticed the ring had disappeared. He was overjoyed and said now was the time to introduce me to Carlo Martini. He arranged for me to meet Carlo at the restaurant. I was so surprised to meet a man I saw almost every day at the post office. I had always thought he was so handsome but never had the nerve to speak to him, since I supposed he was married.

Carlo invited me to go to the Clique Club that Saturday evening for dinner and dancing. Wow, no one had ever taken me for dinner and dancing. I was impressed. We went to the restaurant, and I met so many new people. Those people became good friends and have remained so all my life. The fellows were Joe Sampson, John Tullah, Lee Rieser, and Joe Reger. The gals were Anna Marie Merandi, Marty Reger, Nancy Simons, and Ruth Reger. Faces would come and go, but that group always sort of stayed the same. Carlo was a really good dancer, and I just loved dancing, so we danced the night away. We probably spent at least three Saturday nights a month at the Clique.

We would sometimes go bowling, or party at someone's house, or go to the movies. We both loved movies and would try to catch all the new ones as they came along.

In December 1956, Carlo presented me with an engagement ring. It was a beautiful emerald-cut with baguettes on each side. By now I was so in love with him, I could not do anything but say yes.

THE MARTINI YEARS

Carlo had been raised by his uncle Alfredo (Fred) and aunt Giovanni (Jenny) Fortuna. Carlo's mother had lost her mind after his birth and could not take care of him. Since the Martinis, Carlo's birth family, had three other boys, they asked Uncle Fred and Aunt Jenny to care for Carlo. Having no children of their own, they said they would take him.

He was raised like a little prince. They were good Catholics and taught him all they knew to be a good man. And he was a good man. He was fourteen years older than I, but at the time that just didn't seem to matter to me. He was good to me, handsome as could be, had a great job, had a great car, and knew so much more than I did about life in general.

Carlo had three brothers, Henry, Alberto, and Gino. They all lived some miles away. Henry lived in Martins Ferry, Ohio; Albert up in New England; and Gino in Florida. They were all handsome men. All were married with families.

We had talked to the priest, Father Colombo Bandiero, and his advice to Carlo was to not marry me because he had been married before, and their church did not allow for divorce. Since the Church would not marry us, our friends Henry and Jean Lyons accompanied us to Frederick, Maryland, to be wed on May 7, 1957. Our friends gave us a wedding party and gave us beautiful gifts. All of the Johnsons presented us with lovely things too. The Fortunas had a large amount of friends, all older as they were, but really nice people. They had all accepted me as one of their own and they gave us such really nice things, expensive gifts. I really was so happy to be in the company of all my new friends. The Italian people are a very happy, warm, and loving group. They showered us with attention. I guess they were as excited as Uncle Fred and Aunt Jenny that Carlo had found a suitable wife.

Carlo had a rather large family. There were the Martinis who lived in Martins Ferry. His father, James (Pop) Martini, lived with his eldest son, Henry. There was Henry's wife, Ethel, and his two sons Michael (Mike) and Robert (Bobby). Pop was a lovely old man who took me under his wing right away. I loved Pop! Henry was really nice and would include me in everything. Ethel was a little strange but welcomed me anyway. She seemed to be very nervous and flighty. She always tried to put on a good meal when we went to visit.

Uncle Fred had no family left in America. Pop had been married to his sister, but she had passed on many years before I came into the family.

Aunt Jenny had a large family who seemed to be spread everywhere. There were the Burgesses, who lived in Pittsburgh, Pennsylvania. Her brother Fred lived with his daughter Lena.

Lena was such a cut-up. I just loved her. She would take me shopping in Pittsburgh, and I would wear out before she got through looking at everything, and I mean everything. His son was Fred Jr., and his wife was Blanch ("Tweetie"). They had three children, Patricia, Fred, and Vincent. These were the nicest people ever. And they knew how to cook. Wow, you could really eat hardy up there! They would do anything for you, but you had to be straight with them. If you talked about them, or cheated them, or ignored them, it was almost like a death sentence. They did not understand or forgive betrayal easily.

Aunt Jenny's sister Mary Innamarato also lived in Pittsburgh. Her husband had died before I was married. She had three children, Angelo, Arthur, and a daughter (whose name I can't recall).

Uncle Jim and Aunt Teresa Cacase lived in Weirton, West Virginia. They had a large family. The boys were Fred, Jimmy, and Patsy. Jimmy and Patsy were albinos who ran a bar in downtown Weirton. Fred married Valerie and had several children. I think Patsy got married and had a daughter, Vickie, but I can't remember much about them. The girls were Loretta and Carmelina. Carmelina was married to Vic Prozzi. Loretta's husband had died before we were married.

Aunt Jenny had a brother, James Burgess, who lived in Clarksburg. His wife passed away several years before I became a member of the family. They had a daughter, Lena, and a son, Jimmy. Lena had been married and had two children, Ilamay and another name I really can't remember. She was in a special home for the handicapped . . . .

Uncle Fred Burgess's wife had been a sister to Patsy Canterelli's wife, Ermalinda. Patsy's children Vincent and Frances were great friends with Fred's children Fred and Lena.

I occasionally went to church with Carlo. Although the Catholic church did not accept him or afford him its sacraments, he went anyway, because that was what he had been taught. He was vigilant about his attendance. I had my membership at the First Methodist Church in downtown Clarksburg. I would invite him to go with me once in a while, but he always refused. I sang in the choir, taught Sunday school from time to time, taught Vacation Bible school, and was a member of the church board.

We rented an apartment on Hewes Avenue behind the post office. Our "across the hall" neighbors were the Rossis. We though that was hilarious! It was especially funny since Miss Julia, the eccentric landlady, picked up our garbage daily from the front of our apartment. We would put our liquor bottles in it and thought she would wet her pants seeing Martini and Rossi in her trash cans.

Our apartment was really nice with a furnished living room, kitchen, dining room, small office, bedroom, and bath. We enjoyed it because it was so close to our work places.

It was during this time that the Arcade, on Main Street, burned to the ground. It was a beautiful passageway from Main to Washington Ave. There were shops up and down the sides of the Arcade. Its loss was really felt by the citizens.

In 1959, Dorvett's Tourist home and an adjoining home was put on the market. The tourist home was being sold with all contents. I mean all, even the linens. With Uncle Fred's help on the down payment, we purchased the property. We were able to move in very quickly, since everything we needed was already in the house. We did buy some new furniture from time to time, but a lot of the antique furniture was the kind you just didn't throw away. There were four bedrooms upstairs, completely furnished, with one bathroom. Downstairs was the living room, dining room, kitchen, and pantry. We had the kitchen remodeled, with new oak cabinets. We removed the wall between the kitchen and dining room and added a counter for eating. The pantry became our laundry.

The house next door we rented out. It was a good way to make our payments.

Around 1961, we decided to adopt a child. We had been trying to conceive, to no avail. We applied at the Harrison County Courthouse and was given Genevieve (Gen) Shack as our case worker. We told her we would take one child or a set of twins, if a set was available. My mother, being a twin, made that seem like it would be right. Gen was a good friend of Carlo's, so we felt that would help our case move along faster than those things usually did.

In June 1962, Uncle Fred and Aunt Jenny decided to travel back to Italy for a visit. We took them to New York to catch the boat to Italy. We stayed that first night in the Hotel Emerson. In the morning, I sat up and raised the blinds for light. What did I see but a man standing in an open window in the hotel across the street. He was butt naked. He would put on one piece of clothing and look out at our hotel with his binoculars, and then put on another piece of clothing and look again. This went on until he was completely dressed, even down to his tie.

I couldn't resist and knocked on the adjoining door to Uncle Fred and Aunt Jennie's room. She said, "We're up."

I said, "Look out your window at the hotel across the street."

In a few moments, I heard, "Ehh, ehh!"

Carlo and I laughed so hard at their reaction. We watched while he removed each piece of clothing in the same way he had put them on. Aunt Jenny kept screeching but continued to look.

We went down to breakfast, and I mentioned the episode to the man on the desk in the lobby. He said that happened almost every morning and that they called the police, who would locate the exhibitionist and remove him. What an experience!

After the Fortunas left for Italy, we looked around New York for a day or two. We attended the musical The Unsinkable Molly Brown. It was wonderful. We finally returned to Clarksburg and went back to work.

In August 1962, we got a call from Gen Shack. She explained that our baby girl would be waiting for us at the courthouse in two days. Talk about not sleeping! I could hardly wait.

On that glorious day, we went to the Harrison County courthouse and were ushered into a waiting room. While waiting, I saw a woman carrying a beautiful little blonde-haired, blue-eyed baby through the hall. I remember thinking, Boy is someone going to be lucky. I had made up my mind I would take and love anything they gave me, beautiful or ugly, healthy or sick.

When the lady carried the little girl into our room, she smiled and said, "Wouldn't you like to hold your daughter?"

I gasped and said, "You mean that's our baby?"

She laughed and said, "Only if you want her!"

I held out my arms, and she put a smiling little angel into them. I held her, hugged her, kissed her little cheek, and turned to her daddy and said, "Do you want to hold her?"

He said, "Of course," so I gave her to him. She smiled at him and grabbed his nose. We all laughed. Carlo did have a big nose, and it was handy for her at that time. They explained that there was to be a six-month waiting period before she would be legally signed over to us. We took our treasure home and just looked at her and hugged and kissed her for hours.

We called Uncle Fred and Aunt Jenny in Italy and told them we had a granddaughter for them, Melissa Ann Martini. They were thrilled and couldn't wait to come home. Carlo went back to New York to pick up his parents when they arrived from Italy. They had bought Missy some really nice clothes in Italy. As I remember, among them were a beautiful white woolen coat, hat and mittens, some dresses, and little leather shoes.

They loved Melissa so much and couldn't stop showing her off to their friends.

Carlo and his parents insisted she should be baptized immediately. We chose Lena Burgess, Aunt Jennie's niece, who lived in Pittsburgh, as Missy's godmother, and Luigi Viagnozzi, a friend of Carlo's, as her godfather. Father Colombo Bandiera conducted the service. I felt I couldn't refuse to have her baptized in the Catholic church since my church didn't offer infant baptism, but I told Carlo I would not let her be brought up in the Catholic church. I wanted to take my child to church with me; not have her go to a church that was so restrictive. He did not refuse my demands on this. For her baptism, she wore a little white gown from Italy and her pretty coat, hat, and leather shoes. She was the queen of Clarksburg on that day. Family from Pittsburgh, Weirton, Martins Ferry, Bristol, and Salem, all came to the service and the big dinner at Uncle Fred's afterward.

Living with Carlo and his family was a big happy time. They were always going from one house to another for meals, visiting, and sometimes playing card games. I learned how to understand a lot of their language since they always spoke Italian when they were in groups. I could not speak it, but by just watching and seeing their faces when they spoke, I learned a lot. I loved them all. They were such good people. Oh, they had their prejudices, but so do we all.

In February 1963, we were called to the courthouse to sign the final adoption papers for Melissa Ann. At that time we applied for a boy child. The wait began again. A Mrs. Cook was assigned as our case worker. We waited, hoping for a call soon.

In July or August of that year, Gen Shack called us to say there was a set of twins in Morgantown, but they had been tentatively placed. The woman thought she might be pregnant, and if so, they would not take the twins. So we waited again. In October, Gen called again and said the woman was indeed pregnant and would not be taking the babies. We were overjoyed. On a morning in November we went to the courthouse again to pick up our babies.

They were precious. We named them Christopher Carlo and Amy Lee. They were round little cherubs. Chris had a fuzz of blond hair and blue eyes. Amy had brown hair and dark-brown eyes. They didn't offer much in the way of laughs. They just studied us a lot. Amy, especially, gave us soulful looks.

We arranged for their baptism immediately. Amy wore a little white dress and Christopher wore a white outfit. Father Colombo Banderia conducted the service. Amy's godparents were Frank Merandi and Flora Angotti. Chris's were Chester Ali and Barbara Romano. We again had a big dinner at Nonnie and Nono's, as the kids called Aunt Jennie and Uncle Fred.

When I took them to Dr. Robert Marks for their first checkup, he passed through the waiting room, took one look at them, and pronounced them anemic. They were anemic and allergic to all kinds of things. They had bronchial flare-ups during their first three years. Chris had nine pneumonias and Amy had eight. We finally got them tested, and they were able to be put on allergy shots, which helped somewhat. Amy did pretty well, but Chris still had to be careful of ragweed, feathers, and dust.

I was cleaning his bedroom one Saturday and put him in my bedroom to sleep. I forgot I had feather pillows, and when I got him up he looked terrible. His little eyes were swollen so badly that the whites of his eyes stuck out about one-eighth inch. I rushed him up to Dr. Marks, and he suggested we take him to an allergist in Pittsburgh. We did that and found a medicine that would help. Poor little thing, he took shots so many times. He was a good boy though and put up with it.

The children loved each other very much and played together so well. Missy was the leader, of course, being the queenly type. She bossed everything. When the twins were small, she would take their diapers to the diaper pail and put things away for me. She really was a big help.

I was so proud of the children and would push them around in their twin stroller. Missy would sit in the little carry-all on the back. I would dress the twins in matching clothing, and if I could manage it, dress Missy the same way. I would even take them to town to shop with me. Of course people had to stop and talk about their sweetness.

I recently was at a restaurant with my husband, Jim, and a voice from the past, Jean Sullivan, said, "I can remember walking out of Parsons Souders one day, and hearing singing. I looked down the street and there you were with three little ones behind you. You were singing a little tune and they were marching in a row behind you. It was so cute. I've never forgotten it."

I remember it too. They were probably around three years old at the time. I was probably getting into "teacher mode."

We had a travel trailer and camped a lot in the state parks. We named it "The Martinis and 3 Olives." The kids loved it. We even took the trailer to Virginia Beach and Atlantic City. It was a good savings for us at that time. When we were in Atlantic City, I was painting, sitting on the beach. My canvas blew off the easel and fell into the sand. I was so upset and picked it up to see that the sand added to the dimensions of the canvas. So I got a cup of sand and each time I would get new paint, and I would dip my brush into the sand. It made a lovely picture of the burned-out Steel Pier. I moved onto the boardwalk while I was painting , and a young man came along and asked if he could take my picture.

I asked him why, and he said it would be in the next day's newspaper.

I laughed and said, "Kids, move over, this man is going to make your mom famous." He took the picture, thanked me, and moved away. Imagine my surprise the next morning with our landlord pounding on our door, yelling that my picture was in the paper. And sure enough, there it was. It now hangs on my wall.

Many Sundays, Nonnie would cook a picnic dinner, and we would all go to the Veteran's Park for a picnic. Nono and Nonnie's friends would come, the Felixes, the Minutellies, the Vances, the Scalises, and others. We'd get tables and spread old tablecloths and bedspreads on the ground. Our dinners were always so good, and we really had good times. We'd stay until dark many times, just sitting or lying under the trees. I'd take my paper and chalk and would draw things. The kids would run around, go to the park, get on the swings, etc. No one else brought children, unless someone was watching a grandchild for the day. I seemed to be surrounded by old people, but they were so loving and kind to me I didn't mind.

As time passed, we lost the renter on the top floor of our adjoining house. The bottom renters were thinking of moving also. I got to thinking of a daycare that I might run in the house next door. Plenty of space, bath facilities, kitchen facilities, room for sleep time, etc. I looked into the possibilities, but even forty-five years ago, there were stipulations to be met: physical, financial, educational, healthy environment, etc. After a while, I gave up on that idea and decided to start college for an education in teaching. Carlo agreed, and Nonnie and Nono said they would help by watching the children while I went to day class.

I started by taking one three-hour class at a time. Some semesters I could take six hrs, including a night class, while Carlo watched the children.

In 1963, an oil company wanted to put a gas station on E. Pike Street and asked if we would sell them our houses. We looked around for a house and found one at 144 Jackson Avenue. It was a beautiful old brick home, with eight rooms and a full basement on a large lot. We agreed to sell the houses on E. Pike Street after a time to do some remodeling on Jackson Avenue. We asked Arthur Scalice to put in hot water baseboard heat. He also remodeled the bathroom with tile and new appliances. It was truly beautiful with aqua tiles and new built-in vanity and storage spaces above the bathtub. We had the walls painted white. We remodeled the kitchen by having Stanley Homick build us new cabinets. Arthur did the plumbing. We moved into our new "palace" later that year.

In 1967, the kids were five years old and could go to kindergarten. I enrolled them at the First Methodist Church, and off to school they went. They liked it, and it gave me a chance to get a class in while they were there. When they graduated from kindergarten, I asked Carlo to please go to the ceremony, but he just "didn't have the time." He missed a lot, and they were precious in their white robes and little white hats.

The next year we had to make up our minds about where to send our entire family to school. They were to go to Carlile Elementary School. It was across two lanes of traffic on Pike Street, two lanes of traffic on

Main Street, and they had to cross another street to get to school. We petitioned the board of education to allow us to send them to Towers Elementary School. By doing this, they could walk down Jackson and go up Pike Street to the school. No crossing of six lanes of traffic. The school board agreed and we were very happy. I was a little fearful about them walking five blocks to school, but surprisingly they did really well. Sometimes the girls would come home and report an infraction Chris had committed on the way home, like climbing up on the railing of the bridge that crossed the river so he could look down at the "fish." All in all though, there were never any accidents on the streets. I guess we were always on them about safety, and they took it to heart.

When they were now going to school for an entire day, I could take more classes. I went to the Clarksburg Branch of Salem College, at the Davis Building on Pike Street. I kept working day by day, month by month, semester by semester until I got sixty-three credit hours. At that time I could substitute teach if I wanted to, so I took advantage and taught every grade in twelve different elementary schools in our county over the next few years. Of course I was still taking classes. It was hard to keep everything going-school, housework, occasionally teaching, but I persevered, and in 1970 I took my last semester of a twelve-hour block of elementary education.

I graduated magna cum laude that spring. My family were all so pleased with my accomplishments. It took me eleven years to get my education, but I loved school and didn't resent any part of the wait. That summer I got a call to go to Zeising Elementary School in Zeising, West Virginia. I would teach fourth grade.

I loved teaching. I did some good things with the students. My second year there I had problems with the principal. She could be a lovely lady one day and a devil the next. I did everything I could to please her, but she just couldn't find it in her to be satisfied. I maintained the upstairs bulletin boards, directed a little chorus, and planned and carried out a bicycle rodeo since she thought it would be an educational tool for the school. I entered a leather mosaic my students made in the art fair at Salem College. It took first place. No matter what I did, she was not pleased. Something was always wrong. I didn't follow her directions, or I did too much. That summer I went to the board of education and asked for a transfer. The superintendent said he understood, but I'd need to spend three years in one school before I could transfer. I agreed and sweated out my third year with her.

After that year was over, I again asked for a transfer, and they granted it. I was moved to Alta Vista. I loved it there. I made a lifelong friend, Principal Lucy Anderson. She was so nice and a real cut-up at times. When she laughed, the whole school had to stop and listen. Her laugh was like music. Lucy is still one of my best friends.

Things were not going so well with Carlo and me at this point. Those fourteen years difference in age were becoming obvious in many ways. He wasn't really interested in things I wanted to do. My years of college had opened my eyes to things young people are interested in and do. I had almost made myself act his age so I could get along with him and his family. It was not as if we fought over things, but I just had younger interests. Our intimate life had never been good for me. I sobbed myself to sleep more nights than I care to remember.

My church had installed a new wraparound organ, and it filled the church with sound. It just made you shiver to hear it. I asked Carlo if he would go with the children and me to church to hear this beautiful sound. He refused. It just broke my heart because things the kids and I were sharing, he wouldn't allow himself to join.

I found other interests, and in 1974 I asked him for a divorce. He was shocked and dismayed, but my mind was made up. I couldn't live like that any longer. I asked him to move out and he did. He and his friend Henry Lyon moved all of his clothes out of the house one night and the next day came to pick up his desk and other heavy things. My soft heart really felt sorry for him because he had never been physically mean to me.

He went to the Stonewall Jackson Hotel to live, and the kids and I continued to move on with our lives without him. In 1975, the divorce was granted.

Tiece and Carlo Martini

Tiece, Melissa and Carlo Martini

NONNIE AND NONO'S 50TH WEDDING ANNIVERSARY
1st Row Melissa Ann Martini, Giovannina Fortuna, Fred Fortuna, Mary Innamarato, Teresa Cacase, Amy Lee Martini
2nd Row Christopher Carlo Martini, Authur Innamarato, Carlo Martini, Tiece Martini, Father Colombo Bandiera and Unknown priest.

MY POETRY

This work spans about ten years of my life. I worked in a church or seven or eight of those years, and I think the religious surroundings added fuel to my poetic fire.

I thank God for those days because they helped frame much of my life afterward.

I've had pages in my life, pages of fierce desire to complete works. I had my poetry pages, when I was very young. I wrote my first poem at thirteen. It goes like this:

God's Gifts

The sky is red, the clouds are blue,

One star I see, the moonlight too.

The night is still, the earth at rest,

Our eyes are God's invited guests.

The distant hill, the tall, proud trees,

Their branches stir in soft, warm breeze.

God's gift to us to see and know,

These servants, like us, will come and go.

Let's be like these, with beauty rare,

And take each day as though a dare,

To see and do with God's given grace,

The things that make us winners in this race.

-Meva Threase Johnson 1949

This poem was written on a hilltop across the road from my home. I had carried a pencil and a scrap of paper with me on my walk. The sun had set and dusk was falling. I sat down and regarded the sky. The words of this poem came to me. I took my little pencil and scratched down the words on my paper.

I continued to write poetry from time to time through my twenties, and then I just kind of stopped. One of my favorites I wrote in fifteen minutes while waiting for my ride home from work. I was so bored and impatient and I guess that stress brought on this poem.

Time

Why is it that the clock is so slow when we are ready and waiting to go?

And then it seems that it is fast when we are not wanting time to pass.

Time is the measure of one's life, of all its toils and woes and strife.

It is the thing that makes hair gray, teeth fall out, and minds go astray.

We're in a constant race with time, we're neck in neck and then we lag behind.

Or get overzealous with dreams galore, and change the pace we've kept before.

But remember this-

Time moves steady, her speed doesn't change, she doesn't lag, she doesn't gain,

She keeps the same steady pace while she walks beside the human race.

We're the ones who change the course, who walk like a turtle, or run like a horse.

We're impatient one minute and woeful the next, because we can't change time-

Her speed has been fixed.

-Meva Threase Johnson 1955

I love so many things about the earth. The trees on the mountainside as they sway in the breeze. First at the top of the mountain they will sway to the right. Then the branches on the trees a little further down the mountain will start to sway to the left. This will keep up until the breeze gets to the bottom of the mountain. By that time, the breeze is no longer moving the giants at the top of the mountain. The wind will start to move the foliage in my yard in the same manner. It is so pleasing to watch it all start over again in a few minutes. I spend hours watching; it is like a choir of lovely music. God's hand is so apparent in everything I see and feel and hear.

Clouds

Which of those gliding across the sky

Could be the one in our Savior's eye?

Is it the one with the dragon's tail?

Is it the one with the look of a snail?

Is it the one with the heart-shaped face?

Can any of them find its place?

I know not, but this I know:

I snapped a picture of a stormy sky

And found a baby way up high.

Such a miracle I've never seen

In a place like that, so serene.

It seemed misplaced, but then I saw

Two booties sitting straight and tall.

Could they be waiting to clothe its feet

So it could run to its home so sweet.

God only knows how the face got there,

Giving us a glance of existence rare.

Could it be real or just a dream

Of a life somewhere in its wayward stream?

-Meva J. Scarff 2012

The crickets and frogs at nighttime are like a chorus. In fact, when I was a young lady, I wrote a poem about that sound. Let me share it with you now.

Earth's Music

Music-bubbling water of rippling streams.

Melody of slumbering dreams;

Tune of laughter, beat of tears,

Songs of life and love and years.

To the haunting whistle of autumn winds,

The leaves keep time through hill and glen;

The mountains echo their whispered refrain,

The tales of winter, soon here again.

Birds sing of love to mates on wing,

To keep the world from sorrowing;

At night the stars blink bright above,

The ancient Earth, our gentle dove.

Then winter's here, chilly breezes blow,

Our orchestra, the falling snow;

The tune it plays is soft and sweet,

Until roaring winds it chances to meet.

The music swells, loud and shrill,

It beats and tears with strength to kill;

It howls, it wails, it sobs, it cries,

Then, as it came, it swiftly dies.

The feathered tenor is back again,

And with him, warm sun, his friend;

The flowers waltz, in glowing beds,

They sway and dip their colored heads.

At night, the earthworms glide about,

They hum, they chant and loudly shout;

The happy concerto of tiniest size,

Can make their music float to the skies.

The earth is an opera of music rare,

It can be as fierce as a lion's lair;

Or turn about with grace and ease,

And be a balm with power to please.

Everything has rhythm, most things will rhyme,

If in a given place and time;

Look for music in everything,

And your life will be full of chorusing.

-Meva Threase Johnson 1956

Happiness

It seems to me, this life of ours would so much happier be

If we could only learn to give to those who've less than we.

To give a little bouncing ball or doll baby to a tot

Would take our minds off of our cares and things we've always sought.

Happiness comes from the soul within, it's God's precious gift to us

If we can only learn to use it right, and to Him give our trust.

It is not material things, or things we seek in vain

That make us happy but only the joy of giving and giving again.

We are God's tools in this earthly place,

And we should learn to work,

When he has oiled us with His love

And blessed us without shirk.

He is the "Master of our fates,"

He is the "Captain of our souls,"

And to someone we are these things

With only Him to guide our wayward tolls.

-Meva T. Johnson 1957

How

How can you know, when He says "come"

That you have done what you should have done.

How can you guess, how can you tell,

That what He wants, you have done quite well.

How can you touch, how can you feel,

The pain He bore, when in prayer you kneel.

How can you see, how can you hear,

The things He holds, to be good and dear.

In Holy Writ it says, "love all men,"

Christ did this, and we should follow Him.

How can you know, when the morning breaks,

That you have got, what it really takes.

How can you tell, with each new day,

That you are walking in the proper way.

How can you tell, when the sun sinks low,

That the way you are going, is the way to go.

How can you know, when in sleep you rest,

That He thinks you have done your best.

He said to ask and you would receive.

To trust in Him and always believe.

He'll open the gate, and say come in.

If you do your best, and give your all to Him.

-Meva J. Martini 1959

Spring

What is spring? It is the time of rebirth!

A time of laughing throughout the earth!

Carefree days are here again,

Birds will sing through hill and plain;

Flowers will raise their proud, gay heads,

Wreathed in sunshine in their beds .

Rain will fall, days grow cloudy,

Lightening will flash and thunder growl loudly;

Streams will swell, grass will grow,

And farmers will begin to sow.

This is a sign-what sign you ask?

It is a promise of God's grace,

And forgiving heart for matchless faith.

For all mankind to see and know,

God's love and care makes all aglow!

In Galilee He walked the sea,

Amongst the flowers rained blessings like showers;

He used the beauties of the earth,

To teach us of all love's great worth.

The mustard seed, the lily fair,

The fig tree and wayward tare.

Yes, Spring is here, the earth's reborn,

And we from sinful ways are torn;

To live a life as near like His,

As anyone can say he is.

-Meva Threase Johnson 1955

Funny Thing

Funny thing how the sun brings a bright new day,

Funny thing how it's rays wind their golden way,

To the deep forest glades, to the high windy hill,

To the valleys, and the streams and the daffodil.

Funny thing how the birds seem to just appear,

Funny thing how they know a new spring is near,

How they twitter and sing telling all the earth,

To wake up to the dawn of a new rebirth.

Funny thing how a child's happy smile is brighter,

Funny thing how an aged one's step is lighter,

They can feel in their hearts a new chance for relief,

From the heartbreak of cold, distress, and grief.

Funny thing how a stranger wants to smile,

Funny thing how the world is no longer senile,

How it glows in the face of the warm morning sky,

How it's hopes and aims and dreams are so high.

Funny thing how our Lord was sent down to earth,

Funny thing how He taught us what our lives are worth,

How He begged and pleaded for redemption of sin,

So the beauty and grace of His spring could come in.

Funny thing how He opens our eyes to see,

Funny thing how He makes our hearts pure and free,

How He makes our souls burn with a heavenly glow,

How He makes our tongues talk so the whole world can know.

Funny thing how He loves with undying care,

Funny thing how our lives are no longer bare,

How they're filled for each day with His beauty and grace,

So that all things on earth fall right into place.

Funny thing this big world; funny thing, yes indeed,

It's filled with the humor of life's busy deeds,

Of it's cares, it's loves, it's works and it's prayers,

It's filled with our Lord, with whom none compares.

-Meva Threase Johnson 1956

Love

In all the world, so big and fair,

There is no force so great,

As love divine, as love profound,

As love that conquers fear and hate.

Love so excels the human state,

It goes beyond our reaching,

To heights of glory not conceived,

Yet of our Father's teaching.

He said for us to love Him first,

And then our neighbors as ourselves;

The ones who rend us from our friends,

And feed them hate above all else.

Love is good, for it is He,

Who gave us hope and set us free,

From lowly things that drag us down,

And gave instead a shining crown.

Love is high, above the world,

Of sin and wealth, to which we're curled,

It moves about, as does the air,

And enters into those who care.

It makes us strong to bear the brunt,

Of ridicule and shame and hate,

And looks with pity and goodwill,

On those who would avoid the Gate.

Love makes us glow, from a Flame within,

A Flame that shaped this world of sin,

But twas meant to shelter, clothe, and feed,

The products of His lonely need.

The reptile on his belly slick,

Reversed His good with a lowly trick,

And opened all eyes to the ways of sin,

So that love crept out and hate crept in.

Still His love is strong; for us He cares,

And gives us strength our grief to bear.

A love so great as His deserves

Our all, our hearts, without reserve.

-Meva T. Johnson 1956

Mysteries

As the great waves roll in the ocean,

As the hot sands shift in their beds,

As the white snow caps the tall mountains,

So He looks on those He had led.

While the lusty robin sings in the treetop,

While the fierce lion stalks his prey,

While the busy ant builds his pantry,

We have work to do in our day.

Watch the hot sun feed the wide wheat fields,

Watch the cool rain damp the parched soil,

Watch the soft winds stir the great oak tree,

Watch, if you can, life's mystery uncoil.

See the great forest, stand like a statue,

See the deep caverns, glimmer and shine,

See the huge boulders dot the vast hillside,

See life, in the Master, Devine.

Note the strength and power of the elephant,

Note the alertness and speed of the deer,

Note the craftiness and cunning of the jungle cat,

Note the hurt and hate of fear.

Life rolls, like the ocean, back and forth in doubt and fear;

Truth evades, like the shifting sands, first far, then very near;

Happiness sings, like the robin, if it can pierce the heavy cloud;

Love builds, like the tiny ant, slow and steady and proud.

Joy splatters, like the raindrops, in their carefree, happy way;

Sorrow comes, like the summer sun, heavy and hard to delay;

Understanding is like the cool soft wind, it stirs because we share;

Fulfillment is like the all of earth, it comes from the hand of the One who cares.

-Meva Threase Johnson 1956

During my twenties, I did some summer theatre. A funny thing happened one evening as my friends Barb, Bev, Nina, and I were leaving the movie theater. We passed a small table, and on it were advertisements for tryouts for a new movie being produced by Otto Preminger, one of the most prestigious of all Hollywood producers. Laughingly, we all took one and said we would fill it out and send it in. I looked it over and did just that. I filled out the notice, put a picture of myself with it, and sent it off. When I asked the gals if they had sent theirs in, they laughed at me. Did I really think they would choose me to try out? they asked. Well, yes, I thought, maybe so, why not?

Time passed and we forgot about the whole thing.

In August 1956, I got a letter from Maximilian Slater, assistant to Mr. Preminger, Hollywood, California. I almost peed my pants with excitement. The letter said they were pleased to inform me I had been selected for auditions in the worldwide competition to discover a young actress for the title role in Otto Preminger's film version of George Bernard Shaw's Saint Joan. I was requested to appear for the auditions with Mr. Preminger at the Grand Ballroom, Shoreham Hotel, Washington, DC at ten a.m. on Friday, September 28, 1956. For these auditions, contestants needed to be prepared to play Scene I of Shaw's Saint Joan and also Scene VI , the latter starting with Joan's speech, "Perpetual imprisonment! Am I not then to be set free?"

I took this letter to work with me the following day, and my friends were astonished and dismayed that they too had not sent in an application. However, they were happy for me and watched and waited through my preparations to do the audition. I would walk around the Parish House, where I worked, and recite the lines over and over. My boss would jokingly call me Joan when he walked by my desk. I had great fun just thinking about it and getting ready for that day.

Barbara and Beverly Linsbeck had a grandmother who lived in Alexandria, Virginia. It was only a short distance from her house to the Shoreham Hotel in Washington, DC. Since we went up to Alexandria frequently, it seemed a good place to stay while I auditioned.

We took a Greyhound bus on Thursday, September 27.

When I went to the Shoreham, I was surprised to see perhaps a hundred other girls who had come for the auditions in DC. There were auditions being held all over the United States and Europe. As far as I knew, I was the only person from Clarksburg who auditioned.

The costumes were wild, armor and all. I had considered all sorts of things and finally decided to wear my good suit. It was so pretty, navy blue with a fitted jacket and sailor-hat buttons. I really felt dumb when I saw all the costumes that bespoke the era, but so what? It was my presentation, and nothing I wore would win or lose the day.

We were told to line up by a wall to our right and wait our turn. We moved up as girls came out from the other side of the curtain that had been pulled across the room. You could hear voices and cries of despair from time to time.

When I got to the head of the line, I heard the girl behind the curtain repeat one line, and Mr. Preminger said, "Thank You!"

She cried, "But I didn't even get to say my whole section!"

Again, Preminger said, "Thank You!"

She came storming out from behind the curtain, crying.

I was really nervous but went to my position and was told that Mr. Preminger would listen to my lines and Mr. Slater would prompt me. When Mr. Preminger had made up his mind, he would say thank you, and I was supposed to leave the area.

I was pleased that I was able to recite almost the entire scene VI, before I heard, "Thank You."

My friends and I went away jubilant that I had gotten further than some. The girl who won the part was from Iowa. Her name was Jean Seberg. She did the movie and it was okay, but not topnotch. She did some more work in Hollywood and then went to France, where she became a really big star. Some time in the seventies she took her own life someplace in France.

In 1961 I started college, intending to study education and art. The art classes were wonderful, and I learned to sculpt, doing a self-portrait. I learned to make pottery on the wheel and really enjoyed that. My favorite part was painting in oils. To begin with, I was taught how to sketch things and work with chalk.

Miss Elizabeth Whipple was my teacher, and she was a love. She took her time and helped me along the way. When I got to oils, John Randolph, my cousin, was teaching. He showed me a lot of things that were new to me. By watching him, I learned how to make the canvas come to life. I really enjoyed it, and although I was not really that good, I went on for several years doing oils by brush and palette knife. Most of my work hangs in my home. I've been asked to sell one or two of my paintings, but they are so personal to me that I just can't part with them.

In the seventies, I became very passionate about many things, music being one. I bought an autoharp and learned to play it. I accompanied myself and sang a lot of music during those years. My husband moved out of the house, and I began to date. One friend and I became very close, and he enjoyed talking to me. We got together when we could. It was during this time that I met Jim, and my friend and I parted ways. Jim was all I could think of at that time.

During the seventies I began to teach and spent thirty years teaching students and loving it. I had so much to pass on to the kids, knowledge I had learned from my own life. I tried to teach not only book knowledge but good old common sense. I tried to show the students good morals and love for our fellow man. I believe most of my students really loved me also. Many of them have come to me later and said how much they appreciated all I taught them and the care I took of them. Several have become teachers and attribute the desire for teaching to me and my example. Isn't that a loving presence to have around you? God bless them!

Macel Scarff, Jim and Tiece Scarff
Frances and Glenn Johnson at
Jim and Tiece's Wedding 1975

1st row Jeff, Jim, Lee and Bunny
2nd row Chris, Jim, Tiece, Missy
and Amy at Jim and Tiece's
Wedding October 3, 1975

MY BEAUTIFUL JIM

In 1971, I was hired to teach fourth grade at Ziesing Elementary School in Zeising, West Virginia, about ten miles from Clarksburg. In 1972, I was assigned a student named James C. Scarff. Jimmy was a very serious student and did quite well in class. In 1973, I was assigned his brother, Jeffrey C. Scarff. Jeff also was a good student and very well behaved. He had the most beautiful blue eyes I had ever seen. They looked like cracked marbles. They had prism-like designs in them. As an artist, I looked at everything in different ways. In 1974, I had their little sister Bonita (Bunny) A. Scarff, in my class.

One day Jeff brought a paper bag to school and gave it to me, saying, "Mrs. Martini, I brought something for you." I was surprised and proceeded to open it. In the bag was an egg carton containing a dozen green eggs. I was shocked at seeing green eggs but told him how grateful I was for the gift. He seemed pleased and gave me that little-boy grin. I took the eggs home and threw them away, since I was convinced they must be moldy.

During that same year I coordinated a bicycle rodeo at the school. Jimmy and Jeff both participated, and Jimmy won first place. He was so proud of his accomplishment.

In the spring, we had a spelling bee. Bunny Scarff won the third-grade competition, Jeff Scarff won his competition, and Jimmy Scarff won his. What a family of spellers! I was impressed. After the bee, I conducted the chorus in a few upbeat tunes. In the audience was their father, Jim. Jim tells me he really eyed my miniskirt and my legs as I was directing the music. I remember seeing him there as one of the parents, but that's all there was to it at that time.

At Easter that year, my children Missy, Amy, and Chris were given chicks. As the chicks grew, they became too large for the box we kept them in. What to do, what to do? I remembered that the Scarff boys had chickens at their place-remember the green eggs? So, not being shy, I asked them to ask their dad, Jim, if he knew of any way I could care for chickens in the city. He suggested we build them a pen. Oh sure, build them a pen. Where and how? The boys said their dad would come over and build the chicks a small lot to run in. And he did just that! He brought supplies, fencing, boards, etc.-and built them a lot attached to our yard fence. I was really appreciative and told him so. (Wonder why he would do that for just a teacher? Hm!)

In the summer of 1974, I finally got my transfer to Alta Vista Elementary. It was a real delight.

At that time, I was having big doubts about my marriage, and finally got up the courage to ask Carlo for a divorce.

One day, I ran into Jim at the corner of the Merchant's Bank. We stopped to say a few words, and I told him I was getting a divorce. He said he was sorry to hear that, but he too was getting a divorce.

In May of 1975, my divorce was granted. The children and I stayed in our house on Jackson Avenue.

One evening, I took the kids to McDonald's for supper. Imagine my surprise to see Jim come walking in. How often does a girl look up and see a living, breathing "Viking" in this day and age? That's what I thought I was seeing when he walked in. I'd seen him before, in different settings, but was not prepared for this meeting, which caused my heart to jump into my throat. Wow! My God, he was beautiful! All golden tan, with blond hair and blue, blue eyes that just spoke to you. He was wearing a sleeveless blue shirt that just pumped up the gorgeous male that he was.

Grinning, he asked me what I was doing there.

I said, "Having our supper. What are you doing here?" You know-that little flirty type of conversation we all know how to do!

Well, it seems he was getting supper for his family. After talking for a few minutes, he asked me if I would like to go to a Parents without Partners meeting with him sometime. I asked what that was, and he said it was a group of people who were without partners. They took their kids with them and had a good time.

I said, "Oh no, I'm not going out looking for a man."

He said, "No, really it's just a bunch of people who go out and have dinner and a meeting while our kids play games," and so forth. He said no matchmaking went on. Well, I thought about it for a while and finally agreed to go to a meeting with him.

Sometime later we went to a PWP meeting. Missy, being unhappy with me over the divorce, said she didn't want to go, so I let her go to her friend Berry's house while we went to our meeting.

When we were ready to go home, the children all came out of the room where they had been playing and met up with their parents. I was surprised to see a little girl come out with Jim's kids. When I asked who she was, he said, "She's my youngest daughter, Lee."

Talk about surprised-I had no idea he had four children. She was such a cute, shy little girl though, and

I loved her right away!

We started calling and seeing each other after that. I guess we were both rather astounded at the familiarity we felt. Like finding a lost part of yourself that you didn't know was missing. The first time Jim kissed me was on the knob of land behind his house, right about where our bedroom now stands. When we went anywhere, we took the kids with us. It was hard to have much romance with them around, but we managed nicely. I fell in love with Jim not only for the way he made me feel but because of the way it was obvious he loved and cared for his children. They were everything to him.

He worked an eight-hour job and then picked up his children, wherever they were being cared for, and took them home. He cooked for them, saw to their needs, and took care of the house as well as he could.

In August of that year, Jim received his divorce decree.

We dated through the summer and into the fall. When Jim asked me to marry him, I worried about how I would manage all of the work. I was teaching, keeping house, and caring for my children. Could I take on four more children and a husband? That was nine people to care for. We talked about it and decided we could help raise our families. I said yes! We told our families what we were planning. As I remember, they had little to say, except "good luck." We were married on October 3, 1975. Our wedding was at the Bristol United Methodist Church. It was where I had gone to church all of my growing-up years. Reverend David Reese, assistant minister of the First United Methodist Church in Clarksburg, married us.

My new mother-in-law, Macel, took the girls to her house that night, and my brother and sister-in-law Randy and Pam took the boys to theirs. We had the house to ourselves. That was a real treat in more ways than one.

Jim had decided that four more children would be too many for me to care for at one time, so he suggested we let the girls go stay with their mother in Ohio for a while. Oh, how I hated to do that, but I saw that a slow addition to the family might be best. The night we sent Bunny and Lee off was really hard on Jim. I can still see him trying to fix up Lee's dress and hair before she took off with her grandma. My heart really bled for him.

Jim had a large family. He was one of nine children. One baby, Sonny, had died at eighteen months. The others were Martha, Keith, Robert (Rob), Judy, Dave, Bonita (Bunny), and Richard (Rick). His father, George, had died the year I had Jeffrey in my class. He died relatively young, at sixty-nine. His mother, Macel, was a sweet woman. She lived to age ninety-five.

There are so many stories about Macel and her fears. Macel was afraid of snow on the roads and would not go out if she didn't have to. One time, Jim was driving her to Akron and it was snowing. They came up behind a salt truck and Jim attempted to pass it.

She yelled, "Oh don't pass it, it'll be throwing salt and clearing the road."

Jim being Jim knew his own capabilities and kept going around the truck, much to his mother's chagrin. Coming back, it was still snowing and Jim's windshield wipers quit working.

Jim and Tiece 1976

He had to roll the window down and put his arm out to wipe the windshield. He looked over and his mother was putting her window down. When he asked her what she was doing, she replied, "Well, I want to see too." So she put her arm out the window and made a little hole so she could see what was going on.

When Jim and I started taking square dancing, she said she would like to also, so Chris partnered with her. We went to Salem College and took classes in the science building, and Jim's sister Bunny and her husband, Johnnie, went also. We had such a good time. One evening it started to snow, and I called Bunny and asked her what she thought about going to Salem.

She laughed and said, "You know Mom won't go."

So I called Macel and told her we were going but wouldn't come over after her.

She said, "Of course I want to go. What's wrong with you all?"

So we went over to Wolf Summit, up the long, slippery hill to Macel's house, and picked her up. She never made a sound, but I'll bet she was biting her lip all the way there.

However, she was a strong woman who had done things "the old way" when she raised her children. She washed on a washboard. She put up (canned) hundreds of gallons of garden produce in the summer. She had a strong will but seemed always to be so soft and sweet. Her family adored her.

Back to my story about Jim and our kids.

Jim moved his boys and his belongings to my house on Jackson Avenue. We had to make arrangements about Jimmy and Jeff's schooling. They wanted to continue at Zeising and Gore, until the end of the year. Jane Naylor, a teacher who had taken my place at Zeising, lived a short distance from us and agreed to pick the boys up in the morning and deliver them home at night. My kids continued to go to Central Junior High.

A funny note on Jim's moving. He had tied his mattress to the top of his car and was holding onto the rope from the inside of the car. He was almost to my house when the rope went slack. He looked back and saw his mattress flying down and hitting the road and a car driving up onto it. He continued to drive on because he thought he might get in trouble if he stopped. A couple of guys he worked with came along a few minutes later and saw a woman in a miniskirt crouched down, looking under her car. They stopped to ogle her but did not help. I guess the police were there helping. What is really so funny, looking back on the incident, is that when Jim ties something to a car or truck, he ties it in a death-grip. I guess his mind must have been somewhere else.

We lived on Jackson for three months, but I could tell my love was unhappy not being on his farm. I told him we could move to the farm if that was what he wanted. I could tell he was pleased, and he immediately started fixing up the house on Lambert's Run. It was pretty run down, and Jim had never had time to do much to it since he had moved there. He put down linoleum on the kitchen floor, paneled halfway up the kitchen walls, and papered the rest.. He had previously put up some steel cabinets and a big kitchen sink. He had water installed in the house. (They had been using spring water, and I didn't feel safe drinking that. I know, picky-picky.) Although there were still things needing to be done, we decided to go on out to the farm. Carlo and I sold the house on Jackson, and Jim and I were free to go farming.

After we moved in, little by little, Jim did needed repairs. He paneled the bedrooms and fixed up the bathroom. The house had two front rooms that were connected by a huge double fireplace. We used coal in the front fireplace and it was so cozy.

One evening, I had gone to bed, and a high wind blew up and caused a back draft down the chimney. Jim yelled, and I went running into the living room to see what was wrong. It was hilarious! Jim looked like Alfalfa from the Our Gang Comedy (a.k.a. Little Rascals)-black face with white eye sockets. I couldn't help but roll with laughter. I called the kids to come downstairs. They were shocked to see their dad looking so funny. When they heard what had happened, they bent over with laughter.

Jim didn't think it was so funny though, and he said, "Quit your laughing and help me clean this up."

I looked around. The living room was also covered in soot. It wasn't really all that funny after all. We got everything cleaned up, including Jim, and finally got to bed.

After the back draft, Jim began looking at the chimney very closely. He decided it might not be very safe. After all, it was more than 150 years old. He decided to tear it out of the house. He started tearing down what he could, by hand in the evenings. That meant tearing down walls and sawing out big timbers between the kitchen and the chimney. It took some time to get that done, because he also had farmwork to do in the evenings.

One Saturday, my fixer-up man decided it was time to get out the tractor to pull the chimney apart. He and the boys wrapped a chain around the chimney. I was assigned to drive the tractor because Jim had to be near the chimney to direct when to go and when to stop. He called okay, and I slowly drove forward. It was hard to hear, what with all the noise the tractor made, and when he yelled and waved his arms, I thought I heard him yell go. What he really yelled was whoa. I just kept driving and pulled the chimney right through the living room and ripped our front door out of its walls. When they all yelled stop!, I heard that, looked around, and wanted to run off as far as I could. I knew Jim was just going to kill me. He was disgusted with me but said it could all be fixed, eventually.

The family was not complete without Jim's girls, Bunny and Lee. We took a trip to Ohio and brought them home. After that, our family was really complete. Missy wanted to take Lee under her wing, and Amy wanted to hang with Bunny. The boys were already bonding and things went well. I don't mean things didn't get "up in the air" at times, but we worked with, played with, and loved each other as much as we could.

Our kids had cute little personalities all their own. Missy was our "wild child." She'd always been so busy since she was a baby. Little fingers and feet would just go crazy to move, move, move. She always had a big smile and pert words. Never one to be left behind, she was into everything she could find. She was a real help to me as I tried to keep up the housework. We sometimes would go the Laundromat because I had so many loads of clothes to wash. She would help me load and unload and fold clothes for hours. Twelve loads was not unusual. When Miss was around eleven, she discovered smoking. I have no idea who introduced her, but I imagine it was some friend at school. This was before Jim and I were married. I was so distressed about smoking and her health. I talked and talked to her about it and she would promise to give it up, but I would find out that she had not kept her promise.

One day, I said, "Okay, you want to smoke, you will smoke." So I dragged her to the A&P Supermarket and made her choose Camels. I figured they would be really rough on her throat and she would give up. Back home we went, and I made her go to the basement playroom and smoke every cigarette in the pack. She did and grinned at me. Here I was trying to play good parent-bad parent and she played me. I gave up, and to this day, she still smokes. She quit smoking when she carried her two daughters. They were both premature but grew up to be very healthy.

Amy was so beautiful with her big brown eyes and soft, smooth skin. She was our first artist. She played the piano beautifully. My aunt Margie gave us Grandma Johnson's piano when we lived on Jackson Avenue. It was such a beautiful piece of furniture. Five pedals with Mandolin frets. Amy played on the piano. She was also very sensitive to many things. One time, Jim butchered a pig and brought some of the meat to the house to make sausage. Amy saw that, and the thought and sight did not agree with her. Jim and I went to Wolf Summit to take some of the sausage to his mother. Missy called with an urgent plea to come home. It seemed Amy had gotten sick and broken out with hives. We hurried home and had Amy get into a tub of cool water. I called our physician and he prescribed Benadryl. It took a little while, but finally she recovered. We never let her participate in anything like again. She went on to play the clarinet and oboe in high school. Beautiful music. She was a member of the Liberty High School Band.

Chris was a handsome kid with blue eyes and blond hair. He grew into a tall boy. He would try to keep up with Jimmy and Jeff here on the farm, but it just was not in him. He just was not cut out to be a farmer. He did pretty well in school but did not take part in any after-school activities. He was so allergic to grass and weeds that he couldn't play football. He tried one time when Jim and I were first married, but he just sneezed and got sick, so he had to quit.

One evening Jim shot a crow and hung it on the fence post. It was raining when Chris came home from school.

Jim said, "Hey, Chris, do you see that crow on the fence post?"

Chris looked out the window and said, "Oh boy, can I try to get him, Dad?"

Jim said, "Yes, see if you can get him."

So Chris grabbed a gun and started sneaking out to the barn road. The crow didn't move! He took aim and shot at it. Still it didn't move. He tried once again, and still the crow sat there. Now he was beginning to get suspicious. He sneaked a little closer and discovered what his dad had done. He turned around and shook his fist at the house. We all laughed at his antics. He took it in stride but always was looking for something to get on his dad of a like kind.

Jimmy was a really smart boy with light-brown hair and beautiful hazel eyes. He was always ready for fun. He also was always ready to help his dad. He watched everything Jim did and would repeat that task in a perfect way. He loved to hunt and would sneak off from school to go hunting with his uncle Rick.

I was ill one day and couldn't go to work. I stood in our kitchen window when I saw something move in the weeds on the hill across the road. Living on a country road with very few neighbors, I was concerned about such things. I very carefully went out the back door and up the walk to see if I could find out what was moving. As I got to the end of the smokehouse, I looked down and saw Jimmy's gun sitting up against the rear corner. I immediately knew what was moving the weeds. Since Jimmy got on the school bus earlier than I left for school, he had no idea I was at home.

I called out, "Come on out, Jimmy. I see you over there."

His head appeared above the weeds wearing a shamed face. I asked him what he was planning to do, and he said Uncle Rick and he were going squirrel hunting.

I said, "I don't think so!" He had to call Rick and change their plans. He was not a happy camper that day.

Jeff was such a sweet boy. He had curly light-brown hair and the most beautiful blue eyes I have ever seen. They sparkle like cracked marbles. He was going to be a real catch for some girl someday. His lazy grin and quiet ways were very appealing. He would be up to any orneriness that the others thought up, but he would confess to it if necessary.

When Jeff was in high school, he bought an old Volkswagen Bug. For some reason, it was very hard to start and needed to coast to get started. He made a bargain with his sister Bunny. If she would push it and get it to rolling so he could start it, he would take her to school with him. She did this day after day so she wouldn't have to ride the bus.

He also had a Pinto car. Its horn would blow late at night after the car cooled off. It did this night after night, waking everyone up from a deep sleep. His dad would get up every night and go down and unhook the horn. He finally told Jeff he'd better start unhooking that horn when he came home or he would be awakened himself at nighttime. Jeff didn't do it, so Jim got him up at an ungodly hour to go down and unhook the horn. Finally he got smart and did the task when he got in earlier.

After graduating, Jeff joined the Marine Corps. He did very well in basic training. He fell one day while mopping the floor in his bare feet and broke his right arm. The doctors on base cared for it and put it in a cast. It was not set properly, and he suffered for months with it in a cast. He finally got a discharge from the service because he could not keep up with his buddies with the damaged arm.

Bunny was so sweet and pretty. She was our dark-haired one with almost-black hair and blue eyes. She was quiet but had a temper if pushed. She was a good student and became a flag carrier in the high school band. She also was a runner in track and took honors. Boy could she run!

We were at a picnic at my brother Randy's house one evening and he teasingly said, "I'll bet you I can beat you to that pole!"

He didn't really know how fast she was. They started out, and she left him in her dust. He never suggested a race after that. Bunny went to Elkins to the racetrack to work in the concession stand of our neighbor Ronnie Kimble. She enjoyed working and the money it provided her.

Our daughter Lee was a sweet child. She was so cute with a small face and big hazel eyes. She looks a lot like her brother Jimmy. She was so quiet, you never knew she was there. I would take her to school with me sometimes if I had an opportunity. She would sit in a desk next to me and draw or read or color to her heart's content. We both enjoyed those days.

One day I saw a rabbit across the road and ask her if she could spy it. She looked and said she saw nothing. I couldn't understand it since the rabbit was so visible. I asked her again, pointing to the place where it was.

She started to cry and said, "Mom, I can't see anything there."

When I told Jim about the experience, we decided to ask a school nurse friend of ours to look at her eyes.

Dolly Sumpter gave her an eye test and found that she had 100/20 vision. I was shocked. We took her to the optometrist and found that she was very nearsighted.

We bought her glasses, and I cried when she exclaimed, "Oh, I didn't know what those green things were on the trees." Bless her heart. How could she know?

Lee was always very helpful at home. She would do whatever you asked without complaining. She became more beautiful as she grew. I was so proud of my four lovely daughters.

In 1978, I had a regular appointment with my physician, Dr. Paul Gordon. Dr. Gordon did a pap smear and a vaginal exam.

He said, "Tiece, I'd like to run a few tests on you."

I said, "Oh? What kind of tests?"

He named four or fives tests, and pregnancy was one of them.

I laughed and said, "Now, Dr. Gordon, you've been my physician for more than twenty years, and you know I can't be pregnant."

He just shook his head, and grinned at me, saying, "Well, I feel a little thickened spot, and I just want to be sure of what it is."

So he did some tests and I went home. I didn't say anything to Jim because when we were first married, he had asked me if we should do anything to prevent pregnancy. I told him I didn't think so, since I had been married for seventeen years and nothing had happened during that time.

A few days later, at school, I was called to the phone. It was in the office of my principal, Lucy Anderson. I stood behind her desk when I took the call.

Dr. Gordon's nurse told me all the tests were negative-except the pregnancy, which was positive.

I cried out, "Positive means no."

Lucy punched me and laughingly said, "Tiece, you're pregnant !"

I was so shocked that I couldn't even speak. Lucy was so tickled for me. She and her husband were without children, after years of trying, and she understood.

Jim was working for the board of education, in maintenance. He was serving as custodian that day at Towers Elementary School.

I called him and said, "Guess what?"

He said, "You're pregnant."

I was so shocked he would know. When I asked him how he could possibly know, he said, "I just knew."

It was getting near the end of the day, and Lucy said she thought I should go ahead and take my shaky little self home. So I got in my car and went very carefully-very, very carefully-home. Our road was still mud and it was bumpy. I didn't want anything to disturb that precious little flower I was carrying.

When we told our families, they had different reactions. I especially remember Mother and Daddy sitting on their sofa when we told them. Mother, being her right-out-in-the-open self, said, "That's just what you need, another kid." She loved our baby when she was born though.

When we told the kids, it was even funnier. We planned to tell them at dinner some night, since it was one of the few times we were all together. One evening when we got up the nerve, I asked them if they thought we could make room at our table for someone else, when summer arrived. Remember, there were nine of us at that table already.

When they asked why, I said, "Because we have a visitor coming."

They were enthusiastic and said, "Sure we can put them here at the end, or I will move to the end and they can sit here. Who's coming, Mom?"

I looked at Jim for reinforcement and told them I was having a baby.

They all looked stunned, and then Missy piped up with, "Oh, Mom, you're always teasing."

"No, honey," I said, "not this time. You really are going to have another brother or sister."

Things got very quiet. They all got up and filed off to consider this new phenomenon. From time to time I got questions about the new baby, but as I began to get a round belly, they began to realize I really was telling the truth.

When I went to my obstetrician, she checked me over and said everything looked good. She then proceeded to ask me some questions, the first being if I had considered having the baby aborted.

I was appalled. Did I want to abort my baby? The baby I had begged God for? The baby I had waited for forever? No, I told her, what God had started, He would finish in His own way, good or bad.

She could see my shock and quickly stated, "Mrs. Scarff, I only mention that because of your age. Some older first-time mothers have problems. I would not discourage you otherwise."

Well, I could see her reasoning, since I was then forty-two. But I would not even consider such a thing. It would be a sin in the first place, and in the second place, I wanted to hold my progeny in my arms.

Things went well for me, up to the eighth month. At that time I was pretty big and having trouble getting into small spaces. One day while I was out shopping, I went into MacDonald's to get something to eat. As I squeezed in at that table, my heart started to race. I have a floppy mitral valve, and from time to time it races. I knew if I could find a place to lie down, it would stop. In my panic, I knew of only one place I might get help quickly. Taylor's Used Cars was across the street and the owner was a friend of ours, so I hurried over there.

He had someone take me to my doctor's office. When I arrived there and told them what was happening, they immediately put me on a cot. The racing stopped almost at once.

Dr. Lopez came in and said, "Mrs. Scarff, you should have told us you have this disease."

I said I'd just not thought of it.

She said, "Well, this answers the question of whether to have a natural childbirth. It will definitely be a cesarean."

Truthfully I was pleased, because I was afraid of the trauma of natural childbirth.

I was scheduled to have my baby around the middle of May, but the doctor kept saying, we should wait just a little longer. I felt like I was going to burst, and when she said June 1, I was so happy. Missy insisted she should go to the hospital to see after me. Jim allowed her to go; after all, she was sixteen years old. Pam, my sister-in law, went also.

When I got to the hospital and settled into my room, the nurse came to give me a shot to settle me down. I just stuck my arm out and said the sooner the better.

I had my baby girl at 1:33 p.m. She weighed seven pounds, fifteen-and-a-half ounces. She was twenty-and-a-half inches long. We named her Shawna Lynn. Shawna had dark-brown hair and really dark blue eyes. We were very proud of her. I held in my arms for the very first time and felt as if God had indeed visited me.

My friends Peggy and Vernon Nicholas came to the hospital to see her that first night. My vision was so wobbly that I could see three of each of them. And of all things, when they brought Shawna to me for the first feeding, I asked them to take her back because I could not seem to function properly. I guess the anesthesia was too strong for me and it took me a long time to recover.

When we brought Shawna home, all her brothers and sisters were impressed with her and wanted to hold her. They were really good kids. They helped me with whatever I needed in those first few weeks. Shawna would cry at night, and the only person who could get her to sleep was Chris. He'd take her and walk with her to our bedroom and put her in her crib. She'd be asleep. How, I don't know, but he seemed to have a real bond with her. Thank God!

I really enjoyed the months I had with her at home. I breastfed her for the first six weeks and then she went to a bottle since I was going back to work. Polly Hyre babysat for her for the first year. Polly and her husband, Dave, just loved her and hated to give her up when summer came. I taught school that first year and then decided I wanted to be with her before she grew up. I stayed home for a year and loved every minute of it. She was a real delight. When that year was up, Polly watched her again.

Our children made such a good family, all eight of them. They were good together. They looked out for each other at school. When they came home they always got right into the homework. They helped each other with that too. The boys helped their dad if he needed help, and the girls helped me in the house. I'm not saying they were perfect angels, but to me they were pretty close.

Jim and I occasionally went out on Friday evenings to have a little time to ourselves. The kids would watch Shawna. In later years, Shawna told me the boys would put her in a blanket and toss her up and down. If I had known that, I would have skinned them. I don't think they would have hurt her, but can you imagine such a thing?

Jim's mom and Dad had made apple butter for years as he grew up. He loved it and decided it might be a good project for us since we had such a large group at out table.

We started out by going to Romney, West Virginia, to pick apples. That turned out to be a glorious day of friendships. Lucy Anderson would accompany us many times, and my brother Randy and his family went once or twice I think. Mother went once or twice. We would go up there, pick as many as sixty bushels, load them in Jim's big Ford truck, and come home. Of course we took a picnic lunch and a good time was had by all. When we came home, the apples would be handed out to whomever had ordered some. Lucy would take several bushel, and anyone else who had gone would take their share. What we had left would be made into apple butter.

In the beginning, Jim's family, Macel, Bunny, and Judy; and my family, Mother, Pam, and Patty, would come over and prepare the apples for cooking. Hours of peeling apples, ugh! It was hard, but we talked, ate what I fixed, and had a good time.

After a few years, Jim bought a Victoria strainer. By using this instrument after you have cut your apples into about four to six pieces, you cook them until they are soft and run them through the strainer. It removes the core and skin, which comes out one opening and the cooked apple sauce comes out another opening. It make the long hours of peeling a thing of the past. It took Jim about five hours to do seven or eight bushel of apples.

The next morning, very early, Jim started the fire and put the copper kettle on it. Ten silver dollars, like his dad had used for making apple butter, were lowered into the kettle. The silver dollars kept the applebutter from sticking to the kettle. The applesauce would be poured into the kettle, and a day of stirring constantly would begin.

I would have the task of getting the bottles ready for the new apple butter. I also cooked food for the large amount of people who appear from time to time, during the day, for stirring and tasting. We really enjoyed our apple butter day, and about three or four p.m., we would finally jar all the fruit spread. It would make around fourteen dozen jars of apple butter.

At the old house this was done in the yard, but after we built the new house, we could do the job at the side of our driveway and be close to our basement for eating and resting. We have continued to do this year after year for twenty years. In fact, Jim started doing it twice a year about five years ago. Big money-making project, huh? No! It is all given away. I don't think we eat more than a dozen jars a year.

We have some really good friends who come every year to participate in the big day. Marvin Matthews, Gene Rogers, Dave Scarff, Rick Scarff, and our son Jim all come to stir. Bunny Meredith, Judy Guy, Heather Laulis, and Ron and Sharon Kimble all come to help us jar the apple butter at the end of the day. Our daughters Bunny, Lee, Shawna, and Missy have all helped from time to time.

Jim enters his apple butter at the Salem Apple Butter Festival and many times has come home with the first-prize ribbon.

The apple butter day has become a tradition, and we are known for it all around the county.

Time passed, and the older ones grew up. Missy fell in love with Jeff Hunter, and after she graduated, they were married. She and Jeff had two girls, Chassidy and Brandi.

Amy went to college at Glenville College and met an Iranian boy named Hamid Massoumian Aragai. She showed up at my classroom door one day with this tall fellow with an afro hairdo. She introduced him as Hamid and said they wanted to get a marriage certificate. I was shocked out of my skull. I had never met this young man, he was from a different culture, and what would herd say? I really don't remember the outcome that day, I just know they went back to Glenville, and the next thing I knew, they were married.

Chris dated Grace Randolph. They fell in love and decided to be married. They had a nice ceremony at the Hammond Methodist Church in Clarksburg. They eventually had two children, Kristi and Jonathan.

Jimmy had wanted to go to Ohio and live with his mother when he was around sixteen. We hated to see him go, but it seemed the best thing to do at the time. He graduated from high school in Ohio. Jeff joined the U.S. the US Marine Corp. When he came home, he started seeing Penny Hill, a girl he had gone to school with. They had two girls, Natasha and Amber.

In 1983, Bunny met a fellow named Dave Collett when she was working for Ronnie Kimble at his racetrack near Elkins. She fell in love and was determined to marry Dave. Lee, Shawna, and I went to her wedding in Elkins. I really did not see this as a good thing because we knew nothing about Dave. I cried through the whole wedding. Mr. Collett, Dave's father, promised me he would take good care of our daughter, and I guess he tried to do just that. Bunny and Dave had two children, Josh and Victoria. That left Lee and Shawna at home with us for a few more years. Thank goodness they were too young to leave us for a while.

In 1987, we built a new house on the knoll where we had first kissed each other. Our two hundred-year-old home needed some real work, and we decided building was the best idea. We ordered a home from Grafton Manufactured Homes, and Jim got busy dozing the spot for our new home. He worked many hours clearing, dozing, and moving dirt around to make a sloped yard. He dug the hole for the basement and made it ready for the construction workers to come and build it.

After it was done and the house ready, we waited breathlessly for the meeting of the two parts. On a winter day in early 1987, the trailers rolled in and slid the house on its new basement. We were overjoyed. New house, new kitchen, new bathrooms, new everything. Charlie Knight, a good friend of ours, laid the new carpets. We moved everything from one house to the other shortly after. It was a hard couple of weeks getting everything in place. Truth be known, some things took months being moved.

We had a master bedroom with adjoining bath and master closet. Lee and Shawna had rooms on the other end of the house. They were both given new bedroom furniture sets and were really pleased with them.

We purchased other new furniture for our house and were thrilled with the whole thing.

In 1993, Jim built long cement porches on front and back of the house. They made a nice addition to the whole place. In 1995, he built a four-stall garage on the side of the house. It is connected by a small covered walkway. It makes a nice place for our cars and equipment of all kinds. We clean it out once a year and have our Scarff reunion, which we have hosted for twenty-five years. It is much better than outside, where we used to have it.

In 1989, Dave and Bunny moved to Virginia, and Lee followed them to visit for a while. She met Paul Buczynski, a really handsome and very nice young man. They took the plunge and got married on August 25, 1990, in our backyard. It was a very pretty wedding. They bought a trailer and moved it onto a patch of land across the road from the "old house."

Now we were left with one chick in our henhouse. Shawna was fourteen at this time. She was doing lots of things-going to school, taking dance (which she had been taking since she was about six years old), running track. In her last two years she was really involved with many activities. She worked for Parks and Recreation one summer. The next summer she taught energy express,a federal program meant to enrichen the education of young people. . She was involved with America's National Teenager Production. She went to Marshall University, where the pageant was held. Her dad escorted her to the stage, and she participated in a variety of things Her specialty was dance, and she performed a beautiful one. She took fourth place in the pageant that had about 150 participants. In her senior year, she was captain of the Liberty High School Dance Line, she choreographed the senior school musical of Annie Get Your Gun, was president of the national honor society, and was editor of the yearbook. She graduated in 1996. Our little girl had become a young woman. She was beautiful, outgoing, and very loving.

Shawna had become my best friend through all the years of taking her places and seeing to her needs. She and I could shop, laugh, and confide in each other. Jim and I went to all her games, parades, dances, and performances. People still express the idea that I don't really look my age. I believe this is because I had a child that I had to raise in my later years. She kept me young.

In the fall, she went off to Fairmont State College in Fairmont, West Virginia. She stayed at home for a while but soon found the driving to be too much. I really think she just wanted to have the college life others had. So she rented an apartment (she was holding down a job), and between her money and ours, she made out okay.

When she left our home, she left a void that was very hard to fill. Our last chick had flown the coop.

THE BRONCO

Oh, you wonder, they had a wild steed? No, not really, unless you're speaking of Jim! What we really had was a 4-wheel drive Ford Bronco. It was a blast! Jim used it for everything, and I mean everything. He pushed things, pulled things, chased things, scared things-we might even have made love in it; I don't remember for sure. But it was the all-in-all of vehicles. It was old and rough. Jim made doors out of heavy aluminum. He had chains on all four tires, and horror of horrors, it had only two-wheel brakes.

Regardless, we had all kinds of fun in it with him as entertainer. He would take us up the road on the hill, and then on the way down, he would veer off to the left and take us to a pretty steep drop-off. I don't mean a cliff, but a really steep hill. Down we would go, screaming all the way. We encouraged our friends to go with him for that ride. They all loved being put in danger I guess, because they would always go.

One winter day, we woke to a foot of snow. We had to go to the grocery, and the only way we had was-you guessed it-the Bronc. It did not have a license plate, so we went a back way to avoid traffic. The boys rode in the back all covered up with blankets. On the way, we came upon a man whose car had become disabled on the road. He was walking in that bitter cold, so Jim stopped and asked him if he wanted a ride. He said thanks, and got in the back with the boys. They shared their covers, and we took him to Marshville and let him off. He was appreciative, but I figure he was frozen from riding all that way in the back of the vehicle. The boys never seemed to get cold, but being kids, I guess they made up for it by snuggling.

When it snowed really deep, Jim would fasten a sled to a long rope and pull the kids "'round and "'round in the yard. They loved it. One time he took a barrel and made a path down the steep hill beside the barn road. The kids took a long piece of molded plastic, and using it as a sled, they all got on and rode it down the hill. They screamed with laughter as they went down again and again. It looked like so much fun, and they begged me to get on and take a ride with them. So I climbed on the back, and away we went. When we reached the bottom, it jumped up and then slammed down. Boy, did my head take a pounding. I guess their sled did that all the time, but they didn't seem to mind. I tell you, I sure minded. My head hurt for hours. They hadn't made aware of the little bump they had made, out of snow, at the bottom of the ride. Well, I guess it was all in the way of making me wiser.

Several years before we were living in the old house, some relatives had planted hundreds of pine trees in the meadow on the hill. They were intending to sell them and make a profit. There were still many trees up there when we moved in. At Christmastime, the relatives would come and cut down all the mature trees to sell in town.

They brought them down to the barn lot and left them until they could take them to town.

James C. Scarff
1980

Melissa Ann Martini
1980

Amy Lee Martini
1980

Christopher Carlo Martini
1980

S. Lee Scarff
1989

Jeffrey C. Scarff
1981

Shawna L. Scarff
1996

Bonita A. Scarff
1982

Shawna Lynn Scarff
In her Dance Line Costume
1996

Amy Lee Martini
In her band costume
1980

Bunny in her Band outfit
And her Dad, Jim

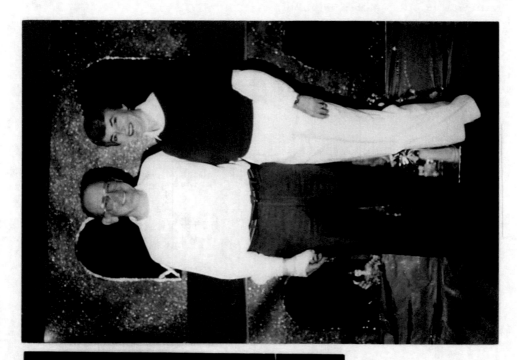

Jim and Tiece

OUR CHILDREN
1st row Missy, Shawna and Bunny
2nd row Amy, Jimmy and Lee
3rd row Chris and Jeff

One afternoon Jim and I were returning from town, and looking over toward the barn, we saw heads moving up and down in the middle of the pile of trees. Jim was furious at the boys for doing such a stupid thing. I think they all felt the switch that night.

Another afternoon, Jim, and Jeff, who was in from the Marines, went up on the hill to fix the fence. Jim backed the Bronco up the hill beside Jeff and Missy's trailer. It had no brakes, so he left it in reverse and turned it off. When he came back, he started the Bronco and thought he could shift out of reverse really fast into second and ease down the hill.

That didn't happen. It didn't go into any gear and just went sailing down the hill, jumped twenty feet of roadway, and landed in the ditch on the other side. It tipped to the side, and Jeff was almost thrown out.

Our son-in-law saw the whole maneuver from his trailer window, and yelled to Missy, "There goes your dad, pullin' a Duke's of Hazard." That was the talk of the town for a long time.

SETTLING IN

Well, our children are all grown now. They have their own lives. Things have happened-some good, some bad, some happy, and some sad.

Missy and Jeff separated while she was carrying Brandi. She continued to live in the trailer right up the hill from our house. She called me one night, very late, and said, "Mom, my water broke."

Being woken from a sound sleep, I was goofy, and said, "Well turn it off and go back to bed!"

She wailed, "Mom, my water broke, and I'm having my baby!"

Boy, that got me on my feet and running.

She was in her seventh month, and this was not expected. I told her to remain quiet and I would call an ambulance, and then I would be there for her.

The ambulance came and they prepared her for her trip to United Hospital Center. When they assessed her situation, they sent her immediately to Ruby Memorial Hospital in Morgantown, West Virginia. I followed the ambulance at an incredible speed since she was on the verge of birth at any minute, we thought.

She lay in bed for nine days before Brandi arrived. She weighed 3.13 lbs. and was 17¼ inches long. When the nurses did an ultrasound on Missy before she had the baby, they saw a thirty-two-week baby with thirty-four-week legs. That worried them, and they were going to call for a doctor until Missy said, "The father is 6'8"."

I guess that explained the long legs. Brandi had to stay in the hospital for twenty-seven days. I would take Missy to the hospital at times and slip into a gown and touch Brandi. She was so beautiful and tiny and expecting a little girl on August 4, 2007. She was with Thomas.

Eventually, Missy moved to Clarksburg with her girls. She is still there and has a fiancé, Chris McGinley.

Chassidy is now twenty-four and has given us our third great-grandchild, Logan Xavier Hess. She and her husband, Jason, have split up and she is living with Logan. Brandi is nineteen and works at Ryans, a restaurant in town. She wants to continue her schooling and become a teacher.

Amy and Hamid had purchased a trailer and put it on our property. They were there for a few years and decided that work opportunities in the area were not good, so they moved to Florida. Amy took a job at the Chalet Suzanne restaurant in Winter Haven, Florida. During this time, she and Hamid moved from place to place, living one summer in a state forest, but after a while parted ways. After a few years, she came home and met Charlie Cook. Charlie is a really nice guy. He had two girls, Cora and Amanda, from a previous marriage. They are very sweet and beautiful girls. Amy and Charlie have two children, Taylor and Devon. Cora married and gave us two great-grandchildren. Amanda is living in South Carolina now. Amy and Charlie live in Hardeeville, South Carolina.

Chris and Gracie split up in 1991. Chris has never remarried. He worked for sixteen years for Southern States Cooperative. After that he drove a tractor trailer for two or three years. He started having trouble with his eyes and had to quit driving. Chris has had eye trouble since he was seventeen. We took him to Johns Hopkins Eye Clinic, and they said he had fungus behind the retina. They had been hearing about it from California in boys who were seventeen or eighteen. They had never heard of it on the East Coast. Since Chris is so allergic to so many things, I wonder if he could have picked it up when Carlo took the kids to Mexico when they were around fifteen. He has what's called acute posterior multifocal placoid pigment epitheliopathy. He was given steroids and the fungus healed, leaving scar tissue behind the retina. It spread to the other eye after some time, and the same medicines were prescribed, resulting in more scarring.

It did not bother him anymore until he started driving trailers into California every week. Then it came back with a vengeance. At that time, he was thirty-six. He went to Ruby Hospital in Morgantown, West Virginia, to their eye clinic. He was again given steroids. At first they worked, but after a while even they stopped working. He is now legally blind. His right eye is completely compromised. The left eye has tunnel vision only. He has other problems and is in pain most of the time. He has recently been awarded his SSI (disability benefits). He lives by himself, and I help him from time to time with going to the doctor or shopping. His sister Missy lives three houses from him, so she goes in and out helping and befriending him. He is a really a fine young man, loving and kind. He has caused himself some problems, but life does that sometimes. He recently became a grandfather for the first time. Kristi had a baby boy named Hunter Allen Lowther. Hunter makes our fourth great-grandchild.

On October 14, 2006, Chris died of a massive stroke. I had known he was very sick but couldn't find any help for it. I suppose if he had gone to a major hospital and had lots of tests, they might have found the clogged coronary arteries on each side of his neck. He, at forty-three years old, was not thought to be in danger of clogged arteries. However, Chris loved to eat fatty foods, was an excellent cook, and made heavy meals. I guess he brought on his own sickness somehow. The doctors at West Penn Hospital in Pittsburgh theorized that small clots must have broken off and been sent to the brain, which in turn caused the stroke.

Jimmy came home from Ohio several years ago and lives in Clarksburg. He met Cheryl Singleton. They were married and moved into her home. She has two boys, Chris and Shawn. They were delightful boys. Things started to go wrong and they divorced. Jimmy lives by himself and works hard at his jobs. He helps his dad on everything he can. I know he feels we are growing older and do not need to do the hard things. He is so sweet to us.

Jeff left Penny's house several years ago and went to Florida. He works for his cousin, Charlie Zook, his mother's brother. He comes in from time to time, but we don't hear from him much. I think he has a girlfriend, but he has never married. We would love to have him up here where we could see him from time to time, but I guess he likes Florida.

Bunny and Dave lived in Elkins, West Virginia. They were divorced in 1998. Bunny and Tori moved to Fairmont, where Shawna attended school. They lived together for two years or so. She was working at Med Brook Medical Center and fainted one night. Her boss expressed a desire for her to have a cat scan. She said it wasn't important and didn't do it. The next night she again fainted and he insisted. She went to United Hospital in Clarksburg and had the scan. She was allergic to the iodine dye and had a bad reaction. They had put her in a bed that had been recently moved and had not been hooked up to the electrical current. She could get no response from the nurses and finally pulled herself to the hall. She called for help and fainted. When they got to her she was really bad off. Her throat was swelling and she was covered with hives. She flatlined and they resuscitated her and started off for the ICU. She started vomiting blood halfway there. It was at that time that they gave her Epinephrine to reverse the dye problem. Bunny has had health problems since.

It was around this time that she met John Kenney. He was from the Mill Creek, West Virginia, and had been a friend of Dave's. They started dating, and he confessed he'd always had his eye on her, but since she belonged to Dave, he had never interfered. They continued to date, and a love affair ensued. We all loved him too, so she had no other option but to marry him. They were married in our St. Mark's Lutheran Church on October 16, 1998.

It wasn't too long after they were married that she discovered a lump in her throat, and after many tests found out she had thyroid cancer. It was removed and she had radiation on it. She goes from time to time to have full-body scans to see about reoccurrence. So far things have been all right with that. She has also been diagnosed with lupus and hypoglycemia.

Josh graduated from high school and joined the US Navy. He was training as a Navy SEAL, but when the Iraq war broke out, his training was put aside. He was stationed in Guam for four years. He came home in July. Tori is a beautiful little version of Bunny and is going into sixth grade in the fall.

Two years ago, Bunny developed a tumor on her lower spine, and in the effort to have it removed for biopsy, a nerve was cut that controlled the right side of her body. She has recovered the use of her arm and hand but cannot lift her right leg. She needs to use a leg lift to pull it into line to walk. She is driving a car again. How I'm not sure, but she is stubborn, like her daddy, and is determined to be well again.

John bought and installed a pool for Bun to use for her exercises. It is so exciting to see her walk and run in the pool, where there is no gravity to hold her down. She says the pool is helping her, and she can now drag her leg a short way. If she keeps working on the muscle, maybe it will get strong enough to take place of the nerve that is missing. We pray that it will be so.

This whole ordeal has been very hard on John, but he forges on because he loves Bunny and wants the best for her and their children. God will bless them with endurance, I know, because He has promised that he will not leave us in vain. She and John and the kids live in Hickory, North Carolina.

Lee, our artist, had a bad time with Paul, and divorced him in 1995. She was working at the Holiday Inn and met a man whom she started seeing. Eventually she and Travis Sutphin were married on December 5, 1997. Tragically, Travis became very ill and had to return to his grandmother's home in the southern part of the state. His mother insisted he and Lee be divorced. They were divorced in 2001. I understand Travis is now confined to a nursing home. His condition has not changed.

Lee was a sad figure for a while. She finally met and married David Hawkins on July 3, 2003. They now live in Hickory. David is a handsome young man who works hard to make things happen. He and Lee hope to become parents one day.

Shawna, our youngest, went to college until her junior year and then decided she needed to get away from West Virginia. She was not meeting fellows who appealed to her, and she missed Bunny. She and Bunny were very close, so she took off for North Carolina. Shawna had been working for a doctor in Fairmont, and one of his patients was a woman named Debbie Floyd.

Debbie had become fond of her, and when she heard Shawna was moving to Hickory, North Carolina, she said, "You must try to meet my son, Jay. He is handsome and single."

Well, Shawna took a job in Hickory at the local Hickory Tavern, a restaurant and bar. One evening they stayed after work and had a party. Jay Floyd happened to be there. She met Debbie's handsome son and fell in love-or lust, I'm not sure. It soon became real love, and they were married. . They have given us our latest grandchild, a beautiful little girl, Gabriella Paige Floyd, on June 11, 2005. Jay has a boy, Shea, six years old, from his first marriage, so Gabby completed their family. In December 2007 they discovered they were pregnant again. Oh, joy of all joys, she was having a boy this time. They named him Cooper James when he was born on September 4, 2007.

Bunny, Shawna, and Lee have all purchased homes in Hickory and have joined the Lutheran Church there, so I feel we will need to spend a lot of time in the south.

We dearly love all our kids. They are spread all over the East Coast, but they come in from time to time to see us. We talk often on the phone.

Jim and I both retired from the school board in 1998. Retirement is pleasant for both of us. Jim is busy on the farm and with the animals. He loves to keep it going. I have worked for five years with Gore Middle School as a liaison for a $21 million grant written by Fairmont State College. I just do the legwork for the site coordinator. It is not hard and I enjoy seeing the students. We are into another grant now, and I've been thinking about quitting the job since our principal, Ed Propst, moved to another position, and our last site coordinator, Julie Gorby, retired. It all depends on how much the new site coordinator can do on her own in her new job. We'll see!

Jim and I often go to Sugar Creek, Ohio, to Amish country. We love it there. We have made some Amish friends and enjoy seeing them and watching them do their "thing." They are fearless people. We enjoy exploring their way of life.

Jim and Tiece resting at Sugar Creek, Ohio

Tiece's School Picture 1976-77

Life is good. God graces us daily with His love. My prayer is that all men can have the same faith and happiness in God that I have.

God bless!

THIRTY YEARS OF TEACHING THE THREE RS

My first real teaching experience was when Mr. Sam Iaquinta called me to substitute at Mt. Clare Elementary. I told him I had no idea how to get there, and he graciously agreed to take me to school. I met him at Krogers Grocery Store, and off we went.

When we arrived, he showed me the inside of the school and the first-grade classroom. I walked into the classroom, and he closed the door behind me. There I was, first time out, first week of school and the first grade. Oh dear God, what was I to do? I had only achieved sixty-three actual hours of college instruction, no teaching skills. But I was allowed to carry out substitute teaching. Was this a mistake?

Think, think, think! Well, every teacher has a plan book, right? Wrong! This teacher had very little of anything in her desk drawers. She would certainly have a list of students, right? Wrong!

About fifteen beautiful children marched into my room at 8:00 a.m.

I said, "Hello," and told them my name. No class list? No problem. Just ask them their names and write them down. That worked, and we were set for the day.

Since I had no plan book, I just asked them what they normally did and they shrugged. So I had to make something up real fast-didn't want to lose their attention. We said the Pledge of Allegiance-stupid move. First graders on the third and fourth day of school do not know the Pledge of Allegiance. Oh well, onward and upward.

I found crayons and paper, so I assigned them some work of some kind, I don't really remember what it was, but knowing my track record of later years, I suspect I asked them to draw a picture of what they had done yesterday. It didn't go too badly; they were kept busy for about a half-hour.

Next thing we did was sing. I chose little songs that all children know, right? Wrong! I had to teach them some little songs. It was fun though and we all laughed and had a good time.

One little hand went up.

"Yes, dear, what do you want?"

He needed to go to the bathroom. Oh darn, it was getting time for a potty break and I had forgotten to ask Mr. Iaquinta where the restrooms were. I lined everyone up and took them to the hall. No restrooms in sight, so I just asked them where the bathrooms were. Every little hand pointed to the windows. I went over and looked, and sure enough, there they were-on the hill. Outhouses!

What fun I was having in Never-Never Land!

We went to the "big potties" and came back to the schoolroom. You know, if I'd had any sense, I would have asked some adult what the score was, but I suppose I was just too embarrassed, so I kept on thinking up games and found a book to read to them, so we played until finally it was lunchtime.

The group and I went downstairs-that's where they directed me-and found some people who looked like they knew what they were doing. Cooks making lunch. Oh joy! We all sat and ate some really good food. I told the cooks how my day had been going, and they laughed their heads off. They apologized but said it was just too funny. They made something really tasty. I can't remember what it was, but they gave me the recipe and I used it a few times.

The day finally ended, and Mr. Iaquinta took me back to Krogers. I thanked him for his kindness and hopped in my car. My family thought the description of my day was the funniest thing they had ever heard. Every time I got a call to substitute, they would tease, "It's not for Mt. Clare, is it?"

Well, I have learned over the years that each new experience is a building of wisdom, so I guess my "wisdom basket" got filled that day.

I continued to sub in twelve different elementary schools and in almost every grade for the next five or six years. It was good money, and I learned far more there about teaching than I ever did in college. Class work does not generate itself, you must generate it. You must move fearlessly around the classroom and ask questions of the students. You must use a smile more than a frown. You need to keep things on a pleasant level, trying to settle disputes quickly and humorously, if possible.

I learned that students are always up to a little fun at the expense of the new teacher. I always chuckled with them. If I ever returned to their classroom, they would remember and be a little easier to handle.

In 1971, I graduated from college and applied to the Harrison County Board of Education for an elementary school teaching job. I was hired right away and assigned to Zeising Elementary School in Zeising, West Virginia.

I met my principal, Frances Rhodes, with another new teacher, Judy Dotson. Judy was assigned the second grade and I was assigned the fourth. Over the years, I have found fourth to be the best place for me, where the kids are just through primary and ready to do real work, yet not far enough along to be real headaches.

Principal Rhodes was a pleasant person, and I enjoyed working with her.

One of my history lessons was on the Native American Indians, Eastern and Western. We always did art work relating to each tribe. I helped my students complete a leather mosaic on a Native American theme. It was really beautiful, a large sunset against a beautiful blue sky. Implements the Indians would use, from pots to papoose boards, were made and glued around on the hillside beneath the sky. Everything on the mosaic was cut from leather that I had ordered from a specialty house. The students would plan their design and cut the pieces out from the different colored leathers. Some of the leather was really hard, almost like shoe leather, so I would cut it out because I was afraid of one of the kids getting hurt. Mrs. Rhodes allowed us to use an old frame that was lying around the school. When the mosaic was finished, we entered it into a craft fair at Salem College. Joy of joys, we won first place!

Mrs. Rhodes was really proud of the mosaic and its award. She bragged about it to everyone and congratulated my class and me on the diligent and beautiful work we had done. Our mosaic was hung in a prominent place for all to see.

At the end of my second year at Zeising, Mrs. Rhodes and I stopped getting along, and I had just about all I could take. I asked my county supervisor to move me to another school, but as I explained earlier, county policy kept him from moving me until I had spent at least three years at my first school.

In that third year, I did some really good things. At the principal's request, I asked the department of state police at Shinnston, about having a bicycle rodeo. I was introduced to Trooper Herbert Richardson as the one taking interest in and setting up bike rodeos. Trooper Richardson showed me how a rodeo was handled and told me what was needed to do one. We worked on this project for a couple of weeks. He came to the school, and we laid out the bike path on the playground. I ordered awards, made out signs, and sent letters home about the big day. The students were to bring their bikes to school that day, if they were going to participate.

The day of the rodeo was bright and beautiful. We had about twenty students participate. There were different skills performed for different ages. The big winner was, you guessed it, a Scarff, Jimmy to be exact. I didn't know it at that time, but he was to become my son in 1975.

When school ended that year, I asked Mrs. Rhodes if I could have the mosaic my class had made, and she said, "No, that belongs to the school."

I saw the custodian from Zeising in town one day and asked him what happened to the mosaic. He said he didn't know, but it was gone. I really believe she took it home.

That summer I again asked for a transfer and was granted one to Alta Vista Elementary in the Broadway section of Clarksburg. I was ecstatic and was given the sixth grade.

Mrs. Lucille Anderson was principal at Alta Vista. She was a very nice lady. She and I became very good friends in and out of school. To this day, she's one of my very best friends.

Alta Vista was so different from Zeising, city school versus country school. For one thing, the students all walked to school. Another thing, the school was a lot newer than Zeising had been. My floor at Zeising was so old and weak that one of my students, who was quite overweight, could make it go up and down as he walked across it. I prayed for the poor little second graders under us, for if that floor ever gave out, they would pay the price.

I had my first Negro children at Alta Vista and learned to love each and every one of them. They were so easy to love. They had a great sense of humor and we laughed every day. They were very skilled runners, and we took great prizes at the county sporting events every year because of them. Others could run, but not with the same stamina! Some of my students I remember, and they stop me to talk from time to time. One boy was Tyrone Lockett. He was really cute and witty. Dana Holyfield was another. I think I attend retired teachers meetings with his grandparents, Mr. and Mrs. Paul Holyfield. I also had Donna Jones, a pretty little girl with a big smile. She is now married to one of my Lutheran friends, Wayne Harman. I also had Preston Williams, whose papa would write Preston's excuses in rhyme. I just loved to get those. So goldarn cute!

The first year I was at Alta Vista, I had a student named Mark Skidmore. Mrs. Anderson told me he had very poor parenting and as a result was very difficult to settle down in school from the beginning. I guess when he was of first-grade age, he would be brought to the front door and would run out the back and hide someplace for the day. This went on for three years, until they finally got him to stay in the school for good. By that time he was nine. When I got him in sixth grade, he was fourteen. Mark read very poorly, and because of that he had a very hard time in almost all of his classes. He was a talented artist and drew while we had class. His grades were very poor, and I couldn't see letting him while away the days and then passing him on, as apparently had been happening. I made a pact with Mark. If he would draw me a representation of what we learned in class, I would give him an appropriate grade for the day's work. He did that, and I was able to give him good enough grades for him to pass.

Mark was ornery and would get into trouble every day. Each day I would drag him into the hall and administer the paddle to his behind. He would laugh through the whole thing. We would talk about the whys of the punishment and he would agree with me. He knew he was being bad and disrupting the class, but somehow he just couldn't do any different.

I went to the restroom one day and left my class doing some kind of work. Since they were right beside the office, I could nod my head and the secretary knew to listen for any disturbance.

When I returned, the kids were just in a state. Mark was hanging out of the second-story window.

I ran over to the window and said, "Mark Skidmore, you climb back in this window."

He said, "No, I'm going to jump!"

I yelled, "Mark, I'm going to have to climb out there and pull you in, and I'm liable to fall and die. Is that what you want?"

"No," he said.

"Then get your silly self back in this window this minute," I fumed.

He came back in and I grabbed him and hugged him. "You're making me gray-haired too soon," I cried.

He laughed and I laughed and forgot about it. What else could I do?

One day we went into the auditorium for some kind of presentation, and I sat with Mark next to me. I couldn't let him sit elsewhere, because he would lead the class into trouble. As I sat there, I began to smell gas. I motioned for the custodian to come to me and told him what I smelled. He went off in search of a leaking gas pipe. As we watched the presentation, Mark would frequently ask me a question. As I turned my head to answer, I was assaulted with gas fumes. It finally entered my mind that the gas I was smelling was coming from Mark. I told Lucy about this and we agreed that we should talk to his parents. His mother said yes, he was, in fact, sniffing the gas in their motorbike.

Things seemed to be getting worse and worse with Mark's activities, and his mother called me one evening. She said he had been stealing little things from Melvin's Market every night. Melvin knew of the activities but just couldn't seem to catch him in the act. One evening though, providence let Melvin see him take a small item, pocket it, and walk out the door. Melvin called the police and they picked him up.

He was taken before the judge, and his mother was told that he would be sent to Pruntytown for confinement unless they could find a reliable person for him to live with. She was dismayed and asked me what to do. The only person they knew who would take him was an elderly aunt, and she thought he was an angel from heaven. She would not be able to handle him. I thought for a while on this and finally told her I thought the best thing would be for him to go to Pruntytown. There he would be confined, would have some schooling, and maybe learn how to settle down. She agreed with me and let him be sent off to Pruntytown.

That summer, I asked my soon-to-be-husband, Jim, if he would take me to Pruntytown to see Mark. We found Mark on the playground. His dad and uncle were both there sitting on a bench. They pointed out Mark and I waved to him. He dropped his head!

I called out, "Mark Skidmore, don't tell me you aren't even going to talk to me after I've come all this way to see you?"

He looked up, grinned, and loped over. He squatted down and dropped his head.

I said, "Honey, how can I talk to you if you don't even look at me?"

He looked up and I hugged him. We took a little walk, and I explained why I did what I did.

He seemed to understand and said, "It's not too bad here, Mrs. Martini. I get good food and have a nice bed. The guys here like me and we get along fine. My dad comes to see me often." He then asked, "Can I come to see you when I get out?"

I said, " Of course you can, Mark!"

Well, we stayed a little while, and I gave Mark some little things I had brought him. Jim and I left and I felt a lot better for having spoken to him. I was afraid he would hate me, but I guess it was not in his little boy's heart to hate someone he knew loved him.

Later in the summer I received a letter from Mark. It was written on a large piece of construction paper. I was amazed to read it and know my Mark had written it. He asked about his friends and told me he loved me. "Please don't tell Ricky I wrote this," he pleaded. Ricky Harper was his very best friend. The letter was circled by Xs and Os. I imagine that someone had to spend hours helping Mark compose the letter, but it didn't matter, he did it for me and I was so thankful.

Each year after I had Mark, he would show up from time to time, opening my classroom door and saying, "Hi, just wanted to see how you are!" We'd talk a little and then he would disappear just as he had appeared.

Several years later, I was doing some summer extra-credit work at Nutter Fort Elementary. When I went outside, I saw Mark doing some yard work. I went up to him and discovered he was working for the city. He was so pleased to see me and wanted to know if I would be there the next day. When he found that I would be there, he said he wanted to bring a piece of art work his daughter had done. The next day he brought a rock that she had used to paint a beautiful scene. I told him how impressed I was with it. He said he thought it was nice and just wanted me to see it. I told him I thought she had probably received her talent from her talented father. His smile was a treasure.

Not more than a year or two after that, he and his whole family were at a summer camp. I guess there had been some card games and drinking going on. Mark got tired and went to bed. His brother-in-law got mad for some reason took it out on Mark. He took a high-powered rifle, went to the bedroom, and shot Mark in his head. When Mark's wife, Connie, heard the gunshot, she starting running toward the bedroom. She met her brother-in-law in the doorway and he shot her too. Such a sad way to leave this world! Mark was a real treasure and I loved him. He was like my child, and now he is gone from me. I pray that some day I might see him running and laughing again in Glory Land.

When Jim and I decided to get married, the students begged us to have a mock wedding in the classroom. What's education for if not to educate? So we said yes. The kids planned it and we participated. I really can't remember what took place, except we said I do. I had lots of fun with those students.

I hadn't forgotten about my mosaic from Zeising, and I just loved teaching about the Indian tribes in our nation. I decided to push in a series of lessons on the Native Americans and do another mosaic. It was a different picture but showed the things the Indians would use in their lives. Each child made a drawing of what he or she wanted, and we traced those on heavy paper. That pattern was used to trace onto the leather what was needed for the piece. I had run low on leather, so I had to fill in some with colored flannel. The kids loved doing this work, and we even made some larger objects, like a jar for holding drinks (it was a two-quart wine bottle, wrapped in leather of different colors), a powder horn (using a horn from one of Jim's cows), a pouch for holding food, a knife sheath, a leather drinking cup, and a purse. Mark Skidmore even made an ax with a leather ribbon hanging from it. This was put on the mosaic. The mosaic was never entered in a contest, but I feel it would have received awards, it was so good. It now hangs in my house.

I had my little angel baby in the summer of 1978. We named her Shawna Lynn. In the fall I had to go back to school, and since my absence had been filled by Keith Athey, I had to teach fourth grade that year. I finally took a leave of absence for 1979–80.

In 1981, a job opening became available at Wilsonburg Elementary, and since it was only three miles from my home, I found myself applying. I was very lucky and was assigned fourth grade at Wilsonburg. Frank Devono was my principal. He was a very good principal, and the teachers at the school accepted me in a loving way. I taught fourth grade at Wilsonburg for seventeen years.

I was now not in a country school, but not quite a city school. It had students from up and down old Rt. 50 and up and down the hollows around there.

I had some really interesting experiences while I was there. I had a set of identical twin boys one of my first years there. They were such handsome little boys, and they were ornery. Chris and Scott Harman. Chris was a little faster in his work than Scott, and Scott would always defer to Chris with a look if he was having a problem answering a question.

One day we were having a discussion, and I asked Scott a question. He looked at his brother as always, and it dawned on me that he was looking at his own chair across the room.

I said, "Scott Harman, what trick are you boys playing on me today?"

His face got red, and the whole class howled with laughter. Here they had traded places just for fun. I laughed with them and told them they would never be able to do that again because I'd watch them more carefully. I not only taught them but their little sister, Julie, and their youngest brother, Brian. Nice children!

Frank Devono was only with us for two or three years, and then he moved to a position in the county office. We were given Rosalee Dolan as our new principal. She stayed with me until I retired. Rosalee was really a nice lady. She was also a wonderful principal. She was caring and impartial. The students knew Mrs. Dolan would treat them fairly. They loved her.

We had a big field by the school, and in the fall and spring, Eilene Travato, the other fourth-grade teacher, and I would take the youngsters out for a game of baseball. We all enjoyed that so much. It was always looked forward to by the kids and the two of us. Many things were learned about each other on that ballfield. Morals were taught on that field, even if we were not supposed to do that. Love and caring were experiences of playing the game. Eilene was a real ball freak and knew the rules. Without her, I would not have done such a good job on the field. And she played for blood. Boy, don't get her mad, she'll have a piece of you! Good years!

Eddie Smith was one of my students. Eddie was lazy and would not really put in the effort to do a good job. When we were working on penmanship, I would put a line of letters on the board and ask the students to do the same on their papers. I would walk around the room while they were working and give praise where deserved.

When I got to Eddie's chair, I usually had to say, "Eddie, I know you can do better if you just slow down and try harder, especially on that small-case M. You know it's supposed to have three "'hills.'"

He would hang his head and try again. It usually always came out as an N. We would practice and practice, and he seemed to get better, but then he'd fall behind when he wrote his name. It would always be Snith.

The year I had Eddie, we did progress reports between report cards. The day had arrived that I had to send one to Eddie's parents because he had some poor grades. I asked if he would bring it to his mother, because he usually got rid of it before she saw it.

He said, "Yes, ma'am, I'll take it home and bring it back tomorrow."

I said, "Are you sure? Because if not, I can give it to your sister Misty to give to your mother."

Well, you would have thought I had lit a fire under his tail because of the way he jumped and carried on. "I said I'll take it home, and I will!" he yelled.

"Okay then, here it is, and take good care of it."

He took it and stomped out of the room.

The next morning, as kids streamed into the room, here came Eddie.

He walked up to my desk and laid his progress report down with a satisfied smile on his face. "I told you, I told you," he sang.

I was overjoyed and told him so.

He stood up really straight, went right to his chair, and got very busy doing something.

I took the report and placed with the others on my desk. Later, when the children were doing a lesson, I pulled the reports up to check them over. When I got Eddie's, I had to laugh.

I said, "Ed, could you please come up here for a moment?"

He gave me a big smile and pranced up to the desk.

I said, "Eddie, you never told me your mother had trouble with her writing. See here? She makes her Ms just like you do! Snith!"

His head almost fell to the floor and he said nothing.

I said, "Maybe we'd better let Misty take a copy home tonight after all. What think you?"

He just nodded yes and crept back to his chair. I had to hold my laughter because it was so funny. Later I told my principal about it, and she too had a good laugh.

But you know, you can occasionally be surprised by some students. When we got into long division, Eddie shined. I usually told the students to remember the acronym DMSB when they were dividing. It stood for divide, multiply, subtract, and bring down. Eddie got it right away, and I would use him as my role model when the others were having problems. I would send Eddie to the child's chair to help him or her, or I would say, "Ed, can you explain how to do this problem?" He would stand up, let his chest swell with pride, and explain the DMSB method. Every teacher needed to have an Ed in their classroom. He was such a dear.

One year toward the end of my career, I taught my granddaughter, Kristi Martini. She lived in the area, and we decided it would be good for her to have me as her teacher. She is a beautiful girl with blonde hair and blue eyes. She was basically shy and had little to say except when asked a question. I don't know how she felt about having her grandmother as her teacher, whether it was embarrassing or not. She always did her best for me, and I enjoyed seeing her every day.

I also had another first for me, a set of triplets, the Elders-Rhea, Stacy, and Leeandra. Stacy and Leeandra were identical twins in the set of triplets. I had never heard of such a thing. Wow, think of that-me not knowing something. They were good students, quiet and studious.

One boy, Sammy Hardman, had a voice like an angel. His mother allowed him to stay up late at night singing with the Davissons, a local country-rock group. I think he told me they were cousins of his. He would sing with them, do his work, and come to school prepared every day. How I do not know. He was a smart young man. I believe he still sings with the same group. I saw him last year at the local Cancer Walk. The Davissons were performing

Teaching at Wilsonburg was a delight. The other teachers were good friends, the students were well behaved, and the parents were nice people. Sadly enough, there were some tragedies. I taught Brandon Clark, a neighbor, in 1996. I taught Leeman Maxwell, a neighbor, in 1995. In 2003, both boys were killed in car wrecks on the road they lived on, Gregory's Run. Brandon made a bad turn into another car at an intersection. Leeman had just received his car and was driving too fast, tried to pass another car, and hit a coal truck head on. I taught a child by the name of Greg Starkey in 1993. When he graduated high school, he joined the military service. While he was on his first leave, he was riding with a friend, who rounded a curve too fast, and hit a telephone pole near the grade school. He was killed instantly. Such horrible loss of young lives.

I supervised student teachers from Fairmont State, Salem College, and West Virginia University. That was a real joy. One of my students was a friend's son, Leslie Reaser. I liked to think that I gave them some real help in achieving their goals.

Several of my students have told me they chose teaching as a career because of my influence on their lives. That is a heartwarming thought.

Mrs. Dolan handed me a page she had received from a teacher named Beverly Fogg. It said, "Mrs. Scarff, after my sixth-grade reading class read The Cat Ate My Gym Suit, they wrote essays about the teacher who has influenced them the most so far in their education. We decided to send the essays out during this special week-National Education Week. CONGRATULATIONS! You have made a difference."

Enclosed was this letter by Scott Morris: "Mrs. Scarf was the teacher who had the most influence on me. One of the reasons was because she had so many different ways of teaching different subjects. I remember one time when I was doing a math problem on the board, and I had to kneel on the floor to finish the problem, and she said, "'I hope you're not proposing to the board.' It was very funny and that is another reason why Mrs. Scarf is my favorite teacher. She gave everyone pieces of candy if you got a one hundred on a test or worksheet. She also made me do my best."

Rosalee placed a little note on the letter that said, "Dear Tiece, this is the highest tribute you could receive. Congratulations! Rosalee."

This "tribute" made me cry to think that little joke made him remember me with such compassion. He was a sweet child.

When you have been closely involved in lives of children for thirty years, you have been given your heaven already. God blessed me with the care of those children and I thank Him daily for it. Those children have made me a better and more patient and loving person. When you're young, you never know where your life will lead you. I had never dreamed of becoming a teacher, but my Master had it all planned for me before I was ever born. What a grand life, what a grand Maker.

I retired from teaching in 1998, as did Jim from his maintenance job. We both enjoy retirement and now can do some things we didn't have time for before.

In 2000, a friend, Ann Leonetti, who attends St. Mark's Lutheran Church with us, asked me if I wanted to do some more work in the schools. I answered that I wasn't quite sure. She taught at Gore Middle School at Gore, West Virginia, some four miles from my home. She said they needed volunteers and wanted to have someone who knew her way around to handle the matter. I talked to Jim about the idea, and he thought it might be a good thing for me to do. It would not take much time, and it would get me out of the house and into what I loved. I think I was getting on his nerves, following him around all the time. I spoke to Ann again and told her I would try it.

I was made chairman of volunteer services and was paid $1500 a semester for the services I provided. I wrote a letter to students' parents, telling them of the need for volunteers. I had about twenty mothers come in to a meeting. I explained what was needed and asked each one to get a TB shot before working around the students. Teachers, also, need to do that every two years.

When all preparations were over, I had about ten excellent volunteers doing things like duplicating tests papers, helping at sporting events, answering the school phone, running errands, etc. It was a good year.

That summer, a vice president at Fairmont State College wrote a Federal grant to prepare middle school students for their futures in colleges of their choices. It was awarded at $21 million for nine counties in West Virginia. The schools were chosen for participation by the free-and-reduced lunch count program. The school had to have a 50 percent or less count. Every middle school in Harrison County was chosen except Bridgeport. The program was called GEAR-UP (gaining early awareness and readiness for undergraduate programs).

To elaborate a bit on my mentioning this earlier, the first year was a big one, and the site coordinators were very busy between their regular teaching duties and running the GEAR-UP program. It was soon discovered that there was too much work for one person at the top in each school. The director and her staff devised a new job, liaison, who would essentially do legwork for the site coordinator.

I was hired to assume the position of liaison at Gore Middle. It would be a ten-hour-a-week job. The basic duties were to print newsletters each month and see that they were distributed to all GEAR-UP students, to help the site coordinator with anything she needed, carry messages and papers back and forth from Fairmont College, and attend meetings twice a month at Fairmont.

GEAR-UP began its first year with seventh--and eighth-grade students. The next year ninth grade would be added. This would progress until the entire high school system was involved. We were actually able to press in another year with the money we had saved the first five years. That took us through the twelfth grade. That was good because we could see what improvements had occurred as compared to the last six-year group.

I was encouraged by Julie Gorby, the site coordinator at Gore, to apply for the job. She was so bubbly and fun to work with, so I applied and got it. I worked the next five years as liaison and applied for the new grant that started in 2006. My work was a little harder, with a small amount of duties added to it for a fifteen-hour job. The pay is good, so I believe I will continue. Gore and Salem middle schools were combined in 2007 on the back lot of Liberty High School. My traveling was only about five miles more, and I was still be able to be with the schoolchildren I love so much.

THE SCARFF FAMILY

Jim's family was large and was scattered over several states. I think I'll just post a little genealogy of the immediate family:

George Edward Scarff b. 7/7/1903 d 12/27/72

Mary Macel (Sutton) Scarff b. 2/23/1908 d. 12/2003

Children:

Herbert Edward Scarff b. 7/7/1930 d.

Martha Evelyn Scarff b. 10/25/32 d.

Keith Edwin Scarff b. 8/6/1934 d. 10/27/84

James Dennis Scarff b. 8/16/36 d.

Robert Franklin Scarff b. 8/24/38 d. 8/26/96

Judith Anne Scarff b. 8/5/40 d.

David Lynn Scarff b. 1/26 /42 d.

Bonita Avis Scarff b. 9/3/49 d.

George Richard Scarff b. 10/28/51 d.

Martha Evelyn Scarff was married to Frank Gump, Bud Aubele, Donald Cash and then Bud Aubele again

Children:

Keith Robert Aubele married Sylvia

    Children: Brendon Aubele

Kevin Aubele married Nancy Fusselman

    Children: Allison Aubele

Keith Edwin Scarff was married to Edna Carpenter, divorced

    Children: Mike Carpenter and Jerri Carpenter

    Carol

    Children: Billy Scarff

James was married to Betty Zook then Meva Johnson

Children:

James Clayton Scarff

Jeffrey Charles Scarff//Penny Hill

    Children: Natasha Scarff, Amber Scarff

Bonita Avis Scarff married Dave Collett and then John Kenney

    Children: Josh Collett and Victoria Collett

Selma Lee Scarff married Paul Buczynski then Travis Sutphin then David Hawkins

Shawna Lynn Scarff married James Micheal Floyd

    Children: Shea Alexander Floyd, Gabriella Paige Floyd and Cooper James Floyd

Robert Franklin Scarff was married to Delores Boring

Children:

Robert Scarff, married Donna Decokse

    Children: Jason Burkhart and Alan Burkhart

    Tim Scarff

    Clifford Scarff

    Elizabeth Scarff

    Jacqueline Scarff

    Rebecca Scarff

    Nathan Scarff

Diana Scarff married Robin Smith and Jeff Marsh

    Children:

    Jeremy, Chad and Alysa Smith and Brittany

Shelley Scarff married Brinton McGarvey and Jason Magalich

    Children: Derik McGarvey, Adam Magalich and Leah Magalich

Thomas Scarff married Sherry Springer and Barbara Bence

    Children: Ashley Scarff

    Tanya Scarff married Tom Shirey and Brad Burkett

Children: Macey , Jake

Judith Ann Scarff married James Guy

Children:

David Guy

James Guy married Kathy LePon

Children: Sydney Guy

David Lynn Scarff married Joan Clawson

Children:

Kimberly Scarff married Glen

Crystal Scarffmarried James Thompson

Kelley Scarff

Candice Scarff married Chris Rudnik

Children: Hannah and Isaac

Bonita Avis Scarff, married John Meredith

Children: Amy Meredithmarried Mitchel Lucas

Children: Chase Lucas

George Richard Scarff married Sharon Hamning

The Scarff Family

First Row: Macel Scarff
Second Row: Bonita (Bunny) Meredith, Martha Aubele, James Scarff
Third Row: David Scarff, Judith Guy, Robert (Rob) Scarff
       Keith Scarff, deceased, Richard (Rick) Scarff, absent

THE JOHNSON FAMILY

Tiece's family was rather close knit and kept mostly to Harrison County, West Virginia.

James William Johnson	b.1868	d.1931
Hattie Lee Holden	b.1872	d.3/1/1950

Children:

Croghan Arnett Johnson	b.11/1890	d. 11/1949
Russell Johnson	b. 12/21/1896	d. 1966
Ila Johnson	b. 1893	d. 1965
Croghan Arnett Johnson	b. 11/1890	d. 11/1949
Marian Frances Owens	b.9/1/1893	d. 4/12/l966

Children:

Glenn William Johnson	b. 8/4/1911	d. 1/17/1985
Hale Everett Johnson	b. 7i/7/1913	d.11/11/1962
Marjorie Lou Johnson	b. 3/17/1925	d. 8/2004
Joey Lee Johnson	b. 11/28/34	

Glenn William Johnson	b. 8/4/1911	d. 1/17/1985
Frances Martha Randolph	b. 2/16/1912	d.1/14/1997

Children

Meva Threase Johnson	b. 1/13/1936
Buddy Hale Johnson	b. 3/20/1938
William Randolph Johnson	b. 6/7/1945
Annabelle Johnson	b. 9/1/1946

Meva Threase Johnson

Carlo Alfred Martini	b.

Children

Melissa Ann Martini	b. 1/29/1962	
Amy Lee Martini	b. 10/25/1962	
Christopher Carlo Martini	b. 10/25/1962	d. 10/14/2006

Meva Threase Johnson	b.1/13/1936
James Dennis Scarff	b. 8/16/1936

Children

James Clayton Scarff	b. 12/20/1962
Jeffrey Charles Scarff	b. 6/5/1964
Bonita Avis Scarff	b. 8/29/1965

Selma Lee Scarff   b. 2/17/1971

Shawna Lynn Scarff   b. 6/1/1978

Melissa Ann Martini was married to Jeffrey Lynn Hunter in 1980, separated in 1988 and divorced in 4/14/60.

Married to Chris McGinley b.

     Children:

     Chassidy Dawn Hunter married Jason Hess, have split up

     Chassidy Dawn Hunter   b. 3/20/81

      Children: Logan Xavier Hess   b. 2003

      Hope Lynn Hess   b. 6/18/08

      Brandy Lynn Hunter

      Children:

     Madison Riffle   b. 7/25/2007

     Lillian Riffle

Amy Lee Martini, b. 10/25/1960, married Charles Cook

     Children:

     Taylor Martini   b 10/9/?

     Devon Martini   b. 6/24/1998

     Cora Cook married Dru Shoff

     Children: Cyrus Shoff

Isabelle Shoff

Amanda Cook

Christopher Carlo Martini, b. 10/25/1960, married to Grace Randolph, divorced

Children:

Kristi Ann Martini   b. 11/1/1986

Children:

Hunter Allen Lowther

Jonathan Grant Martini   b.1/20/1990

James Clayton Scarff, b. 12/20/1960, married Cheryl Singleton, divorced

Jeffrey Charles Scarff   b. 6/5/1962

Penny Hill   b.

Children:

Natasha Scarff   b. 7/27/1989

Amber Scarff   b. 11/6/1991

Bonita Avis Scarff, b. 8/29/1963, married David Collett, divorced

Children:

Joshua James Collett   b.

Victoria Brook Collett   b.

Married John Kenney   b.

Selma Lee Scarff married Paul Buczenski, divorced

    Married Travis Sutphin, divorced

    Married David Hawkins

    Shawna Lynn Scarff b.6/1/1978 married James Micheal Floyd b. 11/24/1972

    Children

        Shea Floyd   b.

        Gabriella Page Floyd   b. 6/11/2005

        Cooper James Floyd   b. 8/25/2007

Buddy Hale Johnson   b. 3/20/1938

married Patricia Lee McIntire   b. 6/2/1938

    Children

        James William Johnson   b. 1/26/1959

        married Ranee Sperry   b. 1961

    Children

        Christopher   b. 1984

        Matthew   b. 1985

        married Jessica Yoke   b. 1985

        Judith Ann Johnson   b. 12/27/1964

married Michael Nolan Wilson   b. 1961

William Randolph Johnson   b. 6/7/1945

married Pamela Lynn Barrett   b. 1/29/1956

Children

Chad William Johnson   b. 1975

married Breeana Marie Dagle   b.1976

Children:

Nathaniel William Johnson   b. 1997

Gabriel Xavier Johnson   b. 2000

Julian Michael Johnson   b. 5/5/2008

Tina Marie Johnson   b. 1977

married Matthew Alan Madrid   b. 1973

Children:

Jenna Marie Madrid   b. 2001

Kinsey Jordan Madrid   b. 2003

Kira Jade Madrid   b. 2003

Anthony Brad Johnson   b. 1980

married Farrah Ann Ford   b. 1982

Children:

Isaac James and Alexander Michael   b. 1/21/2000

Annabelle Johnson   b. 9/1/1946

married Chester Thurlow   b. 1/6/1940

BROTHERS AND SISTERS

1st row Buddy Johnson, Patty Johnson,
    Tiece Scarff
2nd row Randy Johnson, Pam Johnson,
    Annabelle Thurlow, Chet Thurlow,
    Jim Scarff

SIX GENERATIONS OF OIL AND GAS

Nature has provided man with all he needs for a good life. Over the years, some men and women have been able to take the initiative, step right in, roll up their sleeves, and literally pull out of the earth what they needed for a livelihood. Such was the case with my great-great-grandfather Minter Johnson Holden, his son, Hezekiah, and my great-grandfather James William Johnson.

In 1905, Minter Johnson Holden and his wife, Mary Frances (Harbert) Holden, leased their farm to James William Johnson, Minter's son-in-law. Minter Johnson Holden and his son, Hezekiah J. Holden, and James William Johnson formed the Flinderation Oil Company. This land was situated in Ten Mile District, Harrison County, state of West Virginia. It is in the head of Flinderation Hollow, a branch of Salem Fork of the Ten Mile Creek, which flows into the West Fork River.

Minter had bought this farm from his grandfather Peter Holden on October 29, 1869. Peter bought it from the Lewis Haymond Estate on July 28, 1853.

James William (Bill) Johnson was born in Harrison County, West Virginia, in 1868, son of William Croghan and Sarah Ann (Custer) Johnson. Sarah was the first cousin of General George Armstrong Custer. At the age of twenty-one, Bill married Hattie Lee Holden. They made their home in Bristol, West Virginia, and in 1890 had their first son, Croghan Arnett. Six years later, their second son, Russell, was born, and three years later, a daughter, Ila Vivian Johnson.

Bill farmed with his family in Bristol. He was also a teamster. My great-grandmother's younger brother, Hezekiah (Hez), got the craze to drill for oil. The Drake Well at Titusville, Pennsylvania, had been drilled in 1859, and Oil City, Pennsylvania, was founded in 1860. Glorious stories of oil and money undoubtedly filtered to him. His sister's father-in-law had bought a couple of leases and was earning royalties from wells. The thirst for oil invaded his mind and body.

In 1914, he drilled for oil on the family farm. His first well was called the Holden #1. It was a gusher, producing fifty barrels a day. My grandfather dressed tools for his Uncle Hez.

Since the first well was such a success, Hez went on to drill Holden #2 in 1915, but it was a dry hole. This didn't stop Hez, just set him back a bit. In 1916, he drilled Holden #3. It was a good well and produced twenty-five barrels a day. In 1917. Holden # 4 was drilled and was a small well, yielding two to three barrels a day.

Pierce Johnson, my great-grandfather's nephew, lived in Monessen, Pennsylvania. Daddy always said Pierce talked from both ends of his tongue, a trait I believe must be genetic because we are all frantic talkers. Well, Pierce did a lot of talking and bragging about an uncle who had never drilled a dry hole. This inspired men with money to contact Bill, and in 1918, he and Hez went to Pennsylvania. They took, as tool dressers, my grandpa, Uncle Russell, George Lynch, and Earl Gum. They were going to make "black gold" run rivers down mountains.

He drilled two dry holes, and to Pierce's shame, returned home. Pierce's tongue-speed was cut back a bit. Whether this dry hole thing caused it or not, I'm not sure, but Uncle Hez went west in 1918 and never returned. He continued drilling in Kansas and became a wealthy man.

In 1910, Croghan, Bill's oldest son, married Marian Frances Owens. They had four children, Glenn William, my father; Hale Everett; Marjorie Lou; and Joey Lee. In 1917, Russell married Florence Doty. They had three children, Marie Eleanor, Leah Frances, and C. William (Bill) Johnson.

In 1918, Bill was a robust man and had two healthy young sons. They formed a company, J. W. Johnson and Sons, Contractors and Drillers. Drillers at this time made about $12 for a twelve-hour day. In 1919, they bought one-third interest of Hezekiah J. Holden in the Flinderation Oil Company, located in Ten Mile District, Harrison County, West Virginia, for a sum of $900. At this time, Hezekiah Holden lived in Ed Dorado, Kansas.

In October 1919, Bill and his sons Croghan and Russell leased from M. J. Rathbone another 235 acres. The lease at that time was known as the Adams lease on Raccoon Run, Harrison County, West Virginia. With a little backing from his father, Croghan, and his father-in-law, Minter Holden, Bill bought a lease from T. J. Kaufman on Raccoon Run in Harrison County. On this lease, they drilled the Kaufman well two thousand feet to the Maxon Sand. This was a big well, twenty-five barrels a day. With oil selling at six dollars and ten cents a barrel, their odyssey was off and running. The Kaufman was an immense success, and the Carnell of Raccoon Run followed in 1923. It was another success. After the Carnell came the Bramer in 1923, the Swiger in 1923, the Craig in 1929, and the Morris in 1930.

Grandpa and Uncle Russell worked with my great-grandfather pumping and caring for the wells. Besides the pumping, there was always the greasing of the engine, blowing drips, walking lines, gauging tanks, reporting oil, pulling tubing, changing cups, and general maintenance.

It took about two hours to pump the well off from start to finish. Since some of the wells were fairly close to each other, they would start one, let it pump, and start another one. Then the first well would be revisited and shut down, followed by the shutting off the second. Most of these wells were on hillsides, and the traveling would usually be done by foot. Only two or three wells could be done in one day.

Besides drilling, and working wells, J. W. Johnson was interested in the politics of his county. He was a hard worker, and in 1928 ran for sheriff on the Republican ticket. He won the nomination in the primary, but in the general election, he lost to his Democratic opponent, Harry Grimes.

He was interested in his community, and was responsible for the financing and building of the Bristol Methodist Church in 1926. He interested Rev. John E. Hanifan in coming to the church as its first minister. Hanifan later became president of West Virginia Wesleyan College in Buckhannon.

Daddy said his grandfather got very upset watching the school children slush in and out of Raccoon Run, going to and from school. He built a wooden walkway a mile up the hollow for their convenience.

In the early 1930s, Daddy and my uncle Hale started caring for the production, along with Grandpa and Uncle Russell. In 1930, the Johnsons decided to sell their wells. They found a buyer in Midland Natural Gas of Delaware and sold their production for $60,000. After a brief period of time, they found that Midland could not pay, and they had to take everything back. They had been able to realize only the $20,000 down payment.

In 1931 my great-grandfather James William died of a heart attack at the age of sixty-three.

In 1934, Glenn, my father, married Frances Martha Randolph. She was a direct descendant of Samuel FitzRandolph, who settled Salem, West Virginia in the 1700s. Over a period of ten years, they had four children, Meva Threase (Tiece), Buddy Hale, William Randolph (Randy), and Annabelle.

Hale married Helen Donaldson in 1939. They never had children.

Marjorie married Charles W. (Chuck) Greene on August 16, 1947. They never had children.

Joey Lee married Eugene B. Fahey on July 12, 1952. They had a girl and a boy, Janet and Michael.

For twenty years, the four Johnsons ran their production. They bought good producing wells from others. The Sandy was purchased from Haze Morgan. They all raised their families from the revenue of their oil wells. Russell did some dealing with cattle from time to time. But until 1952, they all worked together in oil and gas.

In the early 1940s, Grandpa bought the Rogers on Grass Run for $12,000. The Rogers has proven, over the years, to be one of the best investments the company ever made.

In 1942, Grandfather Johnson had a disabling cerebral hemorrhage and had to give up his labor of love, the oil fields. He continued to advise when possible. Then in 1945, Uncle Russell decided to sell his half share of the company to Glenn, Hale, Marjorie, and Joey for $6,500.

Daddy took my brother, Bud, to work on the Moore, when Bud was just a little shaver. Bud asked if he could get the oil can, which was kept in the water box.

Daddy said okay, and then as an afterthought added, "Well, Buddy, just wait and I can get it myself in a minute."

That minute saved Buddy's life, I believe. Bud was not much taller than the water can, and luckily he did as my daddy told him, because when the box was opened, Daddy found a copperhead snake just in back of the oil can. He killed it and immediately, and saw another one in front of the can. As he killed the second one, a third one flew out of another recess in the box and escaped on the ground. If Bud had tried to get the can, he would have been bitten by at least two or three copperheads and might never have grown to his six-foot, six-inch size. Tell me God was not watching over them that morning! He is always there, if we search for Him.

Daddy took all of us with him to the wells from time to time. We loved going, and in our treks up the hills, Daddy would stop every so often and wonder and talk about the nature he loved so much. I learned the beauty of the earth at my daddy's side. At the well site, we learned about oil wells, snakes, (black snakes are man's friends, killing poisonous ones, like the copperheads), flying squirrels, bees, whittling, poison ivy, etc.

From time to time, we were lifted up to ride the Pitman up and down, or shown how to wash our hands in the crude oil before lunch.

One time, I had gone with Daddy, and while the well was pumping, he went to gauge the tank. To do this, one takes a long stick and drops it into the barrel that holds the oil to see how much has been pumped up that day. Daddy asked me to go with him because he had something to show me. After he gauged the tank with the stick, he told me to come to the edge of the barrel, and pointed out an old tree lying at the bottom of it. He held up the gauge and dropped oil on the tree.

I asked him what he was doing, and he said, "Shh, just watch."

Soon a long black snake glided out and through the spilled oil.

I screamed, and he said, "Be still, or you'll scare her away."

I grabbed his hand and closed my mouth. He said to keep watching, and soon two or three little six-inch-long baby snakes glided after their mother through the slick oil spots. I was thrilled, and he said he kept her as his pet, and played this game all the time. Daddy always forbade anyone to kill black snakes around his wells because they killed off the copperheads.

In 1962, my uncle Hale died, and the work was all on Daddy's shoulders for some time.

As my brothers grew, they were shown how to manage the care of the wells. They worked as Daddy had with his father and grandfather. Joey's husband, Gene, worked for Pennzoil, and had a good working knowledge of the wells. He helps my brother Randy, who now does the pumping and maintenance on the leases. My brother Bud worked for Hope Gas Company, and he too helps out when needed. Gene's son Mike and Bud's son Jimmy are both now learning about the oil business, so they can take care when their time comes. Bud's grandsons Chris and Matt do some general maintenance when needed.

After Daddy retired, Gene took over as manager of the company. My husband, Jim and I, have on occasion helped with oil spills when they were large.

Marjorie Lou kept the books for many years. When she felt she could no longer carry out those duties, Joey Lee took over. Jimmy, Buddy's son, helps her out with specific tasks from time to time.

My brother Randy has two sons, Chad and Anthony (Tony). They are now grown men and married. Chad is thirty-one and Tony is twenty-six, and both are good men. Tony has helped his dad on the LLC doing general lease work.

Randy and his family have developed their own oil and gas company, the J5 Energy. Chad acts as business manager, and Tony, in his own words, is the grunt. Randy helps out in the planning and overall managing.

Bud and Gene retired from their jobs years ago and help out from time to time when needed with the LLC.

We have started leasing our property to oil and gas companies for the drilling of Marcellus wells. They can't produce until they hit the Marcellus sands. They can go two hundred feet deeper to provide a pocket if needed. They can't go into the Utica sands.

Oil and gas has raised three generations of Johnsons and helped raise three others.

From my place, watching and listening, I have enjoyed a special beauty in my life. The working, laughing, fussing, and eventually loving of a family working together is a rare thing. The company has always been a binding aspect of our lives. Without it, we would have ventured away from each other, going here and there for livelihood.

I tell my husband that I would like to go to faraway places to see what they look like, and to experience a different way of living. But he is correct-we have all we need right here: the earth, the sky, the people, and God's love.

ABOUT THE AUTHOR

Meva Scarff is a writer, artist, and singer. She has written a book for teenagers and another for elementary school children. She has worked as a secretary for a judge and an Episcopal minister. She taught school for thirty years. She is the mother of five girls and three boys. She is now retired and living the good life.

ABOUT THE BOOK

Surrounded by Love is a special look into the life of Meva Johnson Scarff. In these pages, she shares anecdotes about her childhood, her school years, her husband, her children, and her shockingly large extended family. She talks about writing poetry and teaching school for thirty years. Teaching was a real passion, and she made the days exciting for her students. Several have said her influence led them to become teachers.

Her life has been filled with fun and laughter, and her overwhelming happiness shines through the words on each page. Join Meva as she shares her life and how she has loved and been loved so deeply.

Printed in the United States
By Bookmasters